Albion Journal

Encounters & Observations

ALBION JOURNAL

Encounters & Observations

ISBN 1-905571-94-1

A CIP record is available at the British Library

First published in 1993 as Journal of the Gallery London
Then as City: The London Journal in 2001

This is a digital format publication
Printed and bound by Blissett: Design.Print.Media
www.blissettdigital.co.uk

Cv Publications
The Barley Mow Centre,
10 Barley Mow Passage
London W4 4PH
www.tracksdirectory.co.uk

Preface

First published as *Journal of The Gallery London* in 1993 with revised editions in 1998 and 2001, over four hundred entries chronicle the life of the city; a powerfully driven arena of dysfunctional experience. Episodes record incidents and encounters; in the streets, with-shoppers and travellers, in the landscape and in scenes of social and internal life.

As the journal develops, fact and fiction blend into a filmic sequence of events. Reality is coloured by a seamless flow of messages of promise and dereliction, gently gathering strands of the communal imagination into a protective shell.

Contents

Part One

Studio-Life

1968 *Redcliffe Square* As the small party continues in the spacious flat an older man enters the front room. Heavily built, wearing cream slacks and an expensive belted tan leather jacket, he ignores the gathering and moves to the window where he stands with his back turned, looking over the square. The coloured girl seems frightened, "You'd better leave now" she advises the company of their unwanted presence.

Canning Town ***"Cheers!"*** The group of revellers greet each other and crash five glasses of beer together, shattered splinters cascading over the floor. A bottomless go-go dancer performs on the bar, picking her way daintily between drinks, in time with the raucous beat of the resident rock band.

1978 *Garbage* The man looks down at the corners of the pavement as he makes his way up to Daventry Street, towards the market in Church Street, and picks up odd scraps of garbage; a torn sweet wrapper, a flattened Coke can. The old woman at the copy centre unwillingly runs xerox from the objects. "It will wreck the glass", she rightly says as she positions the can.

Apartment A recently vacated apartment is strewn with forgotten belongings. Sheaves of magazines clutter the rooms, the kitchen sink is piled high with mouldering tea bags. Pairs of a girl's shoes lie around an unmade bed mauve, red, suede and patent leather, stack heeled. Redundant styles of past years discarded in the hurried removal to another place.

Image in White on Black The artist paints the end wall black and closes brown net curtains of the first floor front room in Paddington. The projector throws up a six feet high news photo of a Belfast soldier's bloodied profile. Taking a small brush dipped in white emulsion he traces some lines around the image. Switching off the projector to gauge the effect the room is filled with a rush of silent voices, of misery, panic and confusion. The pressure is too great, he opens the curtains and returns the wall to white.

Actor Down the passage an actor makes tapes from the TV to practise his actions by, and in another room random collages of music and radio-speak play continuously and at a high pitch.

Commercial Two men and a girl mime with a product. They dance and sing and smile and laugh, energetically but without expression.

Movie The camera moves slowly across the back of the woman's shoulders. She turns her head and tosses her hair. The film judders to a halt. Frame by frame, scratches and dust marks show up on the screen as the film breaks its sequence.

1980

Estate Kids on the corner of the street chuck a missile at the car. The man jumps out enraged to wrestle with them and chase them back into the estate, leaving his companions stranded in the middle of the road.

Spanish Girl

"I like the jazz", says Roza the Spanish model, as the friends sit in the kitchen of her council flat in St.John's Wood after the night class. "I go to the jazz every Thursday night in the Elgin Avenue pub."

Part Two

In Service

1987 *Driver* "I know all the back routes," the driver says as he turns up a side alley by the breaker's yard in Shepherd's Bush, to stick in yet another jam of clever drivers who have thought the same thing.

Night Train Two executives chat conspiratorially about their next month's schedule. "Barry plays these games you know," the sharp faced one says, "he asked me to wait until the end of next week before making my report, and then the bugger only tells the board that I'm not ready to present it yet, and have asked to defer until next month. Don't you worry, I didn't let him get away with that." He looks down as the child from the poor family crawls on the floor and tugs his trouser leg. "Come away Tracy, " says the mother in a pink track suit and denim jacket. The half-caste girl beside her laughs and starts coughing again.

Personnel The girl weeps into the telephone, "Mike, I swear to you on my little daughter's life, I am loyal to you and the firm."

Two Rooms "What can I do?" She says, "I phone the SS all day long. I shift from one room to the other. There's no hot water, the place is a wreck. The landlord's horrible, I've put up with shit from him for too long, and now my baby's ill. I tell them I'd be better off in a bed and breakfast, at least I'd have a permanent address then, and I won't go on one of those big estates either. But they just sit there passive behind the counter. "You'll just have to wait dear," they say, and do nothing about it. I think they forget me from one day to the next." "Perhaps they don't know what to do," her listeners add in sympathetically."There's a waiting list of twenty thousand in Hammersmith. The company nods their heads in agreement and look down in their coffee cups.

Wapping Wall The darkened archway where mechanics work on battered vehicles gives way to the broad aspect of Wapping Wall, and a sense of the river. In a school playground the merry chatter of children on their morning break, while old men pass time seated on benches in the open ground of soaring residential tower blocks. The hand traces fretwork of wire mesh fencing that borders the dusty high road, in which rows of empty styrofoam cups are inserted like a curious kind of listening device, turned towards the dull low lying buildings of the central printing plant.

Artists "A small payment in your post I see, or is it yet another bill?" The landlord's agent converses with the man who stands at the xerox feeding in documents.

"Poor artists, how we pity you with your painful fumblings. I suppose we keep you on out of sympathy, as a minor amusement and distraction on the harsh face of the globe." "As long as we are able to continue to resist imminent submersion from your ever increasing rents." The man replies.

Queue The tall blonde scowls and blows her red nose again. Another, once beautiful, with a haggard expression turns to give a steely glance at two young girls with a pet dog. The line of waiting customers views promotional messages for discount offers up on the screen with indifference. "Can't get up to collect a leaflet?" the commentary continues. The picture shows an elegant lady of mature years seated by her fireside in a large yellow armchair which slowly arises to eject her into a standing position. At the counter a girl with lank brown hair scraped back with a clip sorts an endless stack of envelopes. "*And would it be cheaper if..?*" At another position a man in a red jerkin reaches into an inner pocket to produce a wad of cash packets for accounting. Slow and silent, the queue moves a step nearer service.

Assistant The heavy man with a moustache reaches for a brown paper bag attached to a stack by the till and tears it in half. "Not your day," the customer commiserates. His full carrier bag on the floor tips over and spills its contents. "Seems to be rubbing off on you sir." The assistant observes with a sly smile.

Beautiful Launderette The red button releases the circular door with a snap and the man reaches inside to gather the damp contents. He grasps the sleeve of a shirt and draws out a stream of interlocked garments which disgorge from the machine onto the vinyl floor. He piles them in his arms and forces the garments unwilling into grey garbage bags, spinning the drum to search for the odd missing sock. He pushes past the youth who sits fixed to the bench, staring vacantly at the swirling suds of his wash, and a man in a trilby hat who stands by the door, to lug his bags along the pavement and heave them like boulders into the boot of his car.

The Wedding The guest joins the queue for food and encounters a strange tall cone of profiteroles, coated with a fine web of white sugar. He loses his spoon, which disappears into a bowl of cream, and distracted, dips another in meatballs with pink sauce, to add to his trifle.

Passengers The man removes his overcoat and scarf and folds them neatly on the opposite seat. He makes himself comfortable, brushing specks from his suit, then sits silent looking ahead. He occasionally scratches his nose and twitches, and checks his watch.

The man is in his late forties and wears a dark blue chalk striped suit. He is fair haired and of substantial build. He places his case beside him and opens the snap catch to rummage among documents for his newspaper, then perches a pair of half- frame, gold rimmed spectacles on his nose to commence reading.

An ageing American hippie in a spotted red bandanna and Johnny Reb cap gets on the train, repeatedly tapping his watch to make it work. A slim fair haired boy slips forward and props his head on his hands, his eyes closing. Two Lebanese gentlemen across the carriage discuss their business in lowered voices as the smart city gent on their right loudly crunches his way through a packet of 'Hula Hoops', neatly folding the cellophane in four to put in his briefcase when he's finished.

"Show me the card," says the tipsy girl in a thin lilac dress and gold sling backed shoes, "ooh it's lovely, will you give it to him tonight?" They giggle as they look at the giant picture of a cuddly pet and think of the man. "I'm going to cover it all over with kisses," the girl adds, and they fall about, unsteady in the carriage. A drunk with greased back hair in a brown leather jacket stretches out on the seats. He grunts and shifts his position as the train pulls into another station. The paddies exchange amused glances while women stand over him, annoyed by his selfish and vulgar behaviour.

View from the Train The network of bare winter branches moves away in a windswept avenue, seen through the image of a man in glasses and a grey suit who leans against the screen of the compartment, his paper unread on his knee. The connected door overlays a line of small cottages which sit below the bank of the railway track and recede as it approaches the station at Norbiton.

Gold Circle A fine band catches the light and reflects a brilliant gleam in the gold ring worn in the right ear of a solid girl with close cropped hair, in a black canvas jerkin. She leans against the rain spattered window looking out at the nightlights which ripple in the wet gutter, waiting for the bus to depart from the Richmond terminus.

The Listener As night draws in the increasing quiet is broken only by the distant hum of a passing car, and the occasional squeal of a girl out on a date with a friend, or trapped by a stranger.

Screen The man talks to the camera. His face appears flat and tense on the screen as he tries to imagine the audience to whom he addresses himself, waiting somewhere beyond the dark lens at which he stares. Images shift in layers of brightly coloured film. The insistent sounds of pain and excitement which issue from the box mingle with the clatter of dishes and slamming of the fridge door in the kitchen down the passage, as the man lies relaxed on the sofa in the front room, his feet up blocking the glare of the TV.

Food in Pink and Blue The child looks up shyly as a woman in pink and blue brightly jogs his arm to speed up the action. "And what do you add next? How long does this sit in the oven?" The camera closes in on a saucepan bubbling on the hob as contents of the can are added to a steaming sauce. The woman leans over to smell the aroma and angles her head prettily to encourage the children with eager questions. They reply with correct information precise, polite and noncommital. They continue working at their dishes,handling the implements with care and poise while the woman moves over to another part of the studio to monitor the creation of a sparkling orange summer fruit drink.

Panto The girl gives an enchanting and clear description of the forthcoming Christmas pantomime. In simple terms she describes the plot of the familiar old fairy story, adding cheerful cartoon-style illustrations and useful interviews with the ranks of wide-eyed children who form the cast of the production.

The Prize Experts confer animatedly on the imminent results of the choral event. The winner is announced and a cascade of balloons is released from the gallery to float down amongst the crowd of young girls who leap about squeaking with excitement. A flushed and pretty girl with ruffled fair hair, wearing a red velvet smock and cream lace collar, springs forward lively and cheerful, to receive the prize from a smiling dignitary and carries it back, to be embraced by her cheering comrades.

Decanter Chiselled facets catch the silvery light and give off a mysterious gleam as the decanter is gently lowered to the polished surface of the table top, to be positioned with care adjacent to the massive grey round of a bottle. The brand name is clearly projected for further reference. The brief sequence of a few seconds effectively conveys the quiet and awesome presence of a great cathedral.

Trio A young couple enter the bar. The fair haired girl gives a charming and spontaneous smile as she joins the older woman for a drink. The trio moves over to a side table, and the couple continue their conversation, but the older woman remains depressed and silent, looking ahead of her, just to the left of camera.

Competition The broad bottom of a tired contestant is heaved over the bar of a tall climbing frame in ungainly fashion. She staggers through the water jump and then becomes trapped under a net of rope, her face buried in the mud. A soldier approaches to help and tactfully, the camera moves over to cover another part of the action. She appears again, cheerful and clean in the studio, to complete her part in the competition, to warm applause from the audience.

Carvery "Two slices of lamb on one plate and four slices of lamb on the other." The man in a queue at the carvery instructs a Filipino chef in a tall hat, behind the counter. He skewers the joint and cuts away the fat, skilfully shearing slivers of the bone in a circular fashion with a long serrated carving knife. He shoots a surly glance as the man takes back the plates. Another customer takes his place while he moves on to select from a diverse array of hot vegetables.

Big One A man with a moustache, curly thinning hair and spectacles, sits at an angular table with his cases by his side and raises the block of meat in a bun to take a full bite. His train is announced and rapidly he swallows the remains of the half-pounder. Sweating, his cheeks full and still chewing, he ditches the wrappings and gathers his belongings in both arms to run for the train.

Hardship at Christmas The commentator introduces a sad note at the end of the evening news with a touching story of hardship. His pleasant expression registers concern and sorrow, his smart blue suit an impressive contrast with the creamy powdered complexion of his face.

The Globe A refreshing concoction is poured into the glittering globe of a glass, swirling in alluring fashion round large blocks of ice.

Red Shoes Shapely legs of the model stretch away beyond the view at floor level. Her well turned feet slip into high red shoes placed firm and dominant on the dark polished surface. The angle changes; she switches her mane of curled black hair before going to meet her handsome date as he comes to a door in the far distance. They embrace and her little figure turns on a charming heel as they go out into the bright passage, leaving the room in darkness.

Three Women A group of three women is caught in the bright lights of a shop window. The fair one is comfortably built and wears a white wool wrapover coat with black shoes. Another is dark with a narrow determined mouth. The third, smaller than her companions, in a roll-necked pullover, jeans and high heels. They press forward through the crowd of shoppers, engaged in lively conversation as they make their way to the pre-arranged rendezvous for a social evening.

Figure in a Landscape Along the riverbank a small figure walks away in the far distance. It cuts a sharp black unit against the silver water in the bright morning sunlight.

Dead Can A Coke can lies discarded in the gutter, flattened by the tyre of a passing car.

Vacant Hoarding An empty hoarding stands on the opposite platform of the local station. Flecks of grey and green, remains of many scraped-off posters, circulate and recede in layers. Like fragments of a memory, lost in the infinite space of the black painted panels.

Nightflight The long low rumble of a distant plane spreads to either side of the deep horizon as it makes its night flight to an unknown destination.

The Wind The metal door of the garage with a broken catch bangs intermittently in the night as the great wind gusts through the gardens.

Checkout "Can't you hurry it up?" The old woman complains, standing three people back in the queue. "Whinge, whinge, whinge," mutters the girl at the checkout inaudibly, "Always the same at Christmas - you'll be quicker in the cash queue madam, the next one along." She smiles sweetly at the difficult customer.

Still Two men and a woman sit mournful in the private ward around the girl who lies prone on the bed, all plugged up with tubes and wires, her still face chalked with pan stick and white powder.

Swamp The guide chatters on as the camera drifts over a swamp of waving bullrushes, as he explains the tour of a particular location, somewhere in America.

Deep Blue Light catches a lens of the spectacles and for a moment obscures the eye of the spokesman. The sharp edge of the metal frame contrasts dramatically with the blue backdrop which deepens to violet as it meets the contour of the man's jaw. We move on to a broader picture that includes the interviewer who leans intently towards his subject. The two men converse intelligently on their chosen topic and present an image of elegance and confidence, sustained under the pressure of performance.

Narrow Lane The long cream Jaguar exits from the car park of the supermarket, forcing back a dull blue saloon which winks it breaklights to other cars that all go into reverse. Headlights of vehicles flash and criss-cross in the dark, picking out shapes of late night shoppers who weave in and out of the traffic, pushing loaded trolleys up the narrow lane.

Order "***Fish and chips!***" The man makes his uncompromising order and stands his ground at the counter, waiting for his simply worded demand to take effect. A boy in a light blue pullover plays the fruit machine near the door, prodding the buttons in sequence with the lights. He collects an occasional drop of coins and feeds them back into the slot.

Generator The sun dips between the avenue of trees and casts long shadows over the pathway and the fields. A young man in a blue tracksuit jogs past panting heavily. In the distance a father plays with a football while the children climb the stump of an uprooted tree. Three paths intersect. A girl in pink cycles past a couple out walking their miniature dogs. A generator switches on with a continuous hum behind the high wire mesh fence of the laboratory. The large dish of a radar is seen between blocks of the complex, as families walk out on Christmas Day in their local park.

A Bigger Splash A long billed bird sweeps through the air to dive into the deep clear water. Its flat beak casts up a large splash of foam. Streaks of white spray freeze in slow frame with droplets spreading into the blue void. Beneath the surface shoals of small fishes scuttle to escape the marauding hunter.

The Hunted The soft background music adjusts to a dramatic theme. In a gentle voice the commentator describes the relative strengths of the pretty white bird and the larger black one in pursuit. His tone remains calm and reassuring throughout the kill as he supplies further reasons for the victory of the hunter, analysing in gory detail the sickening incident set somewhere in the Galapagos.

Silent Night A bearded man in a grey quilted jacket leaves the local pub and walks ahead, pausing to light a cigarette before he turns down the narrow lane. The car park of the supermarket stands empty, two trolleys interlocked in the middle of the broad space. A light comes on in a second floor room. TVs flicker behind drawn curtains in the vacant street. The neon red brand name of the store gleams like a beacon the silent night.

Three-Quarters and Profile A girl sits at a small table in the sunlit garden. She drinks and discusses her situation with a handsome young man. She turns and angles her head. Light catches and defines the clean line of her jaw. The well set cheek bones and elegant poise compare favourably with the languid profile of her partner, his wavy blond hair glinting in the sunlight.

Waiting The balding man checks his watch and looks nervously around the club. A girl coughs in the background. He resumes his first position, waiting for the next incident.

Crying The woman stands by the window, her back turned to the light. A man goes over to her and puts a broad hand on her shoulder in a reassuring gesture. She brushes her eyes and gives him a brave smile as she recovers.

Intermix The girl points a gun at the car window and fires every bullet at the seated man. The preface introduces a sequence of rapidly changing bleached out images of a harsh cityscape, over projected with bold titles which announce the popular detective series.

Nightflight-Typewriter The continuous chatter of a typewriter in the office sequence cuts into the long low rumble of the night flight which spreads to either side of the deep horizon, as it makes its way to an unknown destination.

The Bargain A man and a woman grip either handle of the heavy carton as they quickly carry away a bargain sound system from the sale. A bus comes to a halt by a bent-over temporary sign and releases a crowd of eager shoppers from its retracting doors. A man holds back the horde to help an old woman from the step. Girls push their children in buggies, weighed down with bags. A man sits sullen at the wheel of his car, waiting for a break in the stream of people. Through a gap in the hoardings can be seen a great sunken area of excavation. Teams of builders crawl amongst the maze of scaffolding like worker ants as they construct the foundations for the next superstore.

End of the Year "We wish you a merry Christmas and a.." Slurred voices come through the tannoy system in the nearly empty supermarket. "Would Mr... and Mr...kindly come to the Manager's Office, immediately." An anxious voice broadcasts from Customers' Requests.

1988

The Tube A plastic container reclines on the ceramic surface, its attractive design of fine blue divisions with helpful red texts bends in the dips and hollows of finger dents, the light casting pearl grey shadows over the bright white ground. An incisive blue tag signals the seal at the base. The flattened tube of toothpaste becomes an eloquent monument to the past year and provides a welcome continuity as the man enters the bathroom on the first morning of the new calendar.

Rainy Day The woman scuttles along the wet pavement, a child in one hand, the other gripping a loaded bag. A man with a paper exits through the swing doors of the newsagent. A boy, listless, drags an empty granny basket behind him, tripping one foot in and out of the gutter as he goes. The blocks of flats on the estate sit dull red in the early morning light. A speckle of raindrops scatters the pane, half covered by a heavy drape. A bar of light from the window reflects in the eye that surveys looming forms in the shadowed room.

Tempting Pictures are stacked in rows according to size, set on small stands to enable closer study. A watercolour of an alluring girl who reclines nude amidst exotic cushions catches attention. A touching portrait of a fluffy kitten includes useful information of the artist's services on a yellowing typed card slotted in the frame. Romantic landscapes compete with dashing sketches of summer blooms. This treasure trove of beauty makes choice difficult so interest alters to the intriguing display of shoes on offer in the discount sale next door.

New Construction New buildings rise up on the hump of the causeway in blocks of three levels. Light filters through gaps in the construction. A net of scaffolding bars surrounds the steep pitched roofs. Low lying banks of grey cloud give way to cream coloured drifts across the acid blue light from the window reflects in the eye that surveys looming forms in the shadowed room.

Condition The man and woman sit mournful in the private ward, beside the girl who lies prone on the bed, all plugged up with tubes and wires. The doctor talks to them with concern for her worsening condition, as the children bounce up and down, playing before bedtime.

Drone An eager girl crouches by the fence in a big stetson to describe life on the mid-western farm. Voices drone on behind her in a chorus of the familiar folk song.

Boy Rooftops of crumbling old buildings and ranks of tower blocks slip by, seen through the reflection of a fair haired by in a grey and green bomber jacket who sits in the far seat of the carriage.

Paint Store A diagonal section of brickwork has fallen away from a small shed with corrugated roof, revealing a store of brooms, old signs and paint tins on the platform at New Cross.

Lunch Break "£2.99 change sir, and enjoy your meal." The small coloured girl serves the customer quickly and he removes his tray to sit at a twinette table next to a smart young man with black creamed hair. They sit straight-backed, shoulder to shoulder, munching silently and staring ahead. Cheerful workers invade for their lunch, skinny office juniors jostle in the queue. Laughter arises from the group near the windows. Across the room a girl with a broad pockmarked face and heavy fringe takes a hefty bite from her bun and continues chatting animatedly to her friend. A Big Bernie in a classic grey wool overcoat sorts the day's schedule with his partner. "Now, take the load away up to the stockist and don't forget to make him sign for it.." "Makes you want to eat as fast as you're served" the man attempts to converse with his neighbour, who just then crumples his carton and departs, leaving the man to concentrate on his regular portion of fries, unsalted.

Cross Connection The ticket collector sucks remains of a pack of Ribena, his hat at a jaunty angle as he leans back on a tall stool in his booth. Crowds pass through the barrier into Liverpool Street. ***"My Horror by Victim"***, declare the news stands. The message fades in a fresh downpour. Ahead a fair haired girl in a blue velvet jacket and long skirt opens a bright green umbrella and picks her way carefully between brown puddles, to reach the ramp downwards to her mainline connection.

Garbage The tall blonde girl becomes agitated with the man and sweeps angrily from the house. She drives away in an elegant fast car. He runs out to persuade her to stay. A pile of chicken bones is transferred from plates into a small bin, with thoughts of tying up the full garbage bag and placing it outside, but the man returns instead to the front room to watch the rolling credits of the glamorous series.

Banana A banana is raised to the mouth as blurred forms of yellow and brown come into focus in a subtly conceived shot, that reveals an old man struggling forward, bent under a heavy load. A car passes on the wet road outside as the hand approaches the switch to cut the detailed account of harvest problems in the particular country.

The Jeweller A man with greying moustache and gold-rimmed spectacles leans forward over the counter to adjust the position of clocks and bracelets in the dark window of his little shop. Next door heavy girders arise out of the new shopping centre under construction, behind a row of green painted hoardings, covered with a line of dramatic posters of unknown performers.

Buzzing The red-bearded tinker sits at the base of the escalator, his wife, child and belongings beside him. "Buzzy, buzzy," he repeats to their great amusement and hunches his shoulders, imitating the robotic commuters who move in closed ranks up the stairway.

Doughnut "Give me that doughnut, I must keep my strength up," the girl with chopped blonde hair in a black roll neck and leather skirt chats to the sensitive Chinese boy who serves her in the office canteen. "I've got orders from seventeen customers to complete, twenty metres of fabric to print this month." The phone rings and the boy accounts to his anxious employer, listing the seven sandwiches which remain in line on the counter cased in neat plastic containers, as yet unsold.

Silent Pitted grey and black layers of bark twist along the surface of the mildewed trunk. Round sections of wood lie by the uprooted stump of a tree. A man rolls away one of the cuts for firewood. A neighbour catches him as he walks along and converses "Nag, nag, my wife and sister go on.. "Why don't you ever go out?" They say, so I did." The man continues along the path silent, turning the section over with his foot.

Mission '**For All Peoples**', the message is engraved in Roman letters on the portico of the grand building. Worshippers leave their gathering and circulate amiably outside the mission. Traffic stretches away in a long line down the hill and brake lights wink in the darkness on the slow route towards Clapham South.

Object of Desire A girl strides into the darkened room. She is dressed in a severe fashion, a grey suit, black stockings and high heels. The temperature must be high, for, in spite of the cool look of the interior, she removes her hat and jacket to relax on the sofa under an overhead fan. She loosens her blouse and shakes out her long dark hair, peeling back the silver wrapping of the chocolate bar to bite off a chunk with pearly white teeth. She licks her lacquered lips, eyes dreamy with contentment. In the darkness another mouth also waters for the object of desire.

Man of Action The lean and craggy features tense as the head turns slightly to the right side.A forefinger touches the left cheek as a pensive mood overtakes him. The eyes, normally hard and penetrating, betray a nervous quality unusual in the man of action.

White Goods In the brightly lit interior of the discount store is displayed a glittering array of TVs, tape decks, ovens, microwaves, radiators, electric kettles, hoovers and teasmades, which stretch in a grand parade of temptation down the length of the store. A lean and smartly turned out assistant whistles snatches of the popular disco hit playing through speakers as he hops onto a step to polish the chrome edged door of one of the products on offer.

Flotsam The river has subsided from the heavy rains of the past two days. Breaks in the bank are marked by a scatter of white flotsam, pebbles, branches and sundry garbage, cast up over the sandy track. A fisherman glances nervously over his shoulder as the cyclist passes, anxious not to be soaked by deep puddles in the muddy track.

View from the Hill Substantial properties nestle amidst the winter trees below the green slopes of Richmond Hill. In the far distance can be seen a small car park by an industrial plant. Twin chimneys of the power station break the skyline near Kingston. Birds drift slowly overhead in the fresh breeze. The broad wooded landscape recedes in pale bands to a grey horizon, interrupted by odd clusters of red roofs and power lines. Sunlight picks out three sharp white blocks of skyscrapers, over on the right near Kew.

Power Station Criss-crossed masts of boats pulled up under tarpaulins by the marina glint in the afternoon sunlight. Groups of fishermen huddle under large green umbrellas, their noses poked red through balaclavas.

Children run in and out of the tall beech trees which line the avenue. Men in kayaks row side by side, battling the current. To the left great chimneys of the power station rise above deserted buildings, shielded by a thin line of poplars. Graffiti marks the arch by the bridge with records of bygone assignations, scattered in the underpass to Kingston.

Clearing Heavy blue rainclouds pass over the darkened slopes of Wimbledon Hill, broken by long streaks of silver green. Above the clouds puffs of grey and white disperse into a clearing sky.

Waiting "Most unpleasant, yes." A snatch of conversation drifts over from the opposite platform. The man looks down and adjusts the belt of his beige raincoat with particular attention, slotting the tab through its loops and centring the belt buckle. He arranges his lapels and checks for an even drop of material, then stands waiting for the train, his briefcase between his feet.

The Listener The passenger rests his gaze on the silhouette of a rubber plant in a single lit window out in the darkness. A girl with thick curled fair hair extinguishes her cigarette and sits bored, a green corduroy bag on her knee. Scratched sounds emit from the headphones of the boy who listens to tapes in the next seat, as the travellers sit silent in the train, halted on the track between suburban stations.

Part Three

The Resort

Villefranche-Sur-Mer 18.06.88-31.06.88

Waiting The fat man in a long yellow shirt and white shorts shifts from one foot to the other as he awaits his partner's service. Below the apartment a young woman in dark glasses and a white dress stands still by the door, waiting to be collected by her companion to go for a walk.

Conversation The young girl smiles at her friend and consumes another mouthful before continuing a confidential conversation, at their lunch together on the balcony.

Still Life with Reflection Three bread rolls remain in their cellophane packet, positioned beyond two white bowls adjacent to an open book, some cutlery and a carton of apple juice. The arrangement is seen again in the heavy glass of the sliding door, along with the reflection of a woman and child seated at the table.

At the Pool A heavily built bearded man pulls himself up from the pool, grunts and shakes himself, passing a hand through his dripping hair before padding off to find a towel.

Walking A man with brown tinted spectacles parks his car at the side of the quiet avenue and rests against the window. The visitor glances at the black and gold security gates to a private villa and down at the long reddish leaves scattered in the gutter by the open end of a drain. At the top of the hill a three way junction indicates ***Nice-Menton-Monaco***. Streams of fast moving vehicles jockey for position with motorcycles on the dusty route. Further along a woman with two companions. She walks by smiling, with short cut black hair, wearing a soft wool pink tracksuit and gold chain necklace. One of her escorts tall, fair haired and bronzed in a white singlet and shorts. The other man, heavier and bearded, with dark curled hair.

Watching A man stands in the gardens to observe as his child wanders towards a neighbour's apartment. He returns inside, then comes out to resume the same position, smoking a cigarette while his wife awaits further developments, standing hidden behind a trellis screen by their door. He checks by signal with the neighbours for their tolerance of the situation and turns to reassure the woman. He exhales smoke from the cigarette and surveys the plants, while maintaining a watchful eye on his child at a respectful distance.

Midday A man sucks at a peach. He leans forward to let the excess juice drip onto the beach. He stretches and turns about, uncomfortable on the pebbled surface in the midday heat.

Incident A dachshund cocks its leg against the bag of a woman reading on the promenade at Cannes. The owner seizes her pet and moves rapidly away from the unfortunate incident. The girl stands up furious and marks the guilty party's route to a beachside restaurant with a steely glance.

On the Train In the close heat of the carriage the woman tries to cool herself, fanning the air with a piece of paper. At the next stop two more ladies seat themselves, squashing her further into the corner and continuing their conversation oblivious to her increased discomfort.

Continental Conditions A block of writing paper flattens a mosquito against the plate glass sliding door, to the child's great amusement.

White Light A tall German family in matching sportswear stand by their grey saloon, shading their eyes against the glare bouncing off white asphalt in the car park. A mechanical digger on the nearby construction site comes to a halt for a midday break. A workman settles on a low wall to examine his lunchbox in the dusty area beside the tennis court.

Coin 'Liberte-Egalite-Fraternite', the engraved message is enhanced by a single stem of leaves crossed by a sheaf of corn. The ten centimes coin, designed by A.Dieudonne and L.A.Griffour, is turned between the thumb and forefinger, surveyed in closeup during the afternoon siesta.

View with Interior A young cypress nestles close to the pink and white apartment block. A ground floor window is protected by a decorative metal grill. White wood trellises and small bushes separate the gardens. A drying towel is draped over a plastic chair on the tiled patio, seen through the heavy sliding door to the ground floor room. A child's shoe and book lie discarded on the blue divan, beneath a framed sketch of spring flowers and beside a conical metal lamp.

Whistling A heavily built man in blue and lemon patterned shorts stands with a cigar permanently clamped in his teeth, batting a ball back and forth to a young girl. In the nearby construction site a mechanical digger clatters away at the rock face. A girl whistles as she returns from her trip to the pool.

Playing A girl in cerise top, white layered skirt and round pink hat, taps a ball back to her brother as they play in the gardens in the late evening. Families sit out on their balconies at the end of the meal, chatting and watching the deepening blue of the hills surrounding the resort.

New Day A bird skims over the plantation of young trees, seen against cream clouds and pale blue sky of the early morning. Sprinklers play over the gardens. A train passes in the embankment and the mechanical digger starts up at the rockface in the nearby construction site, its insistent clatter backed by the continuous hum of a generator.

Takeaway "Une double cheeseburger et frites grand pour emporter", the visitor requests. Streams of young girls in smart blue and white striped uniforms busy themselves at the cash desks, urged to fast delivery by their managers in crisp white shirts and pressed navy trousers. At a single table a pretty blonde turns away a lock of hair from her face and sips a Coke, gazing at her companion as he clears his order. A group of lanky American kids invades the restaurant, draping themselves around the eating area. The lively crowd is seen before a colourful mural depicting an old French harbour town. An elegant woman sits with her daughter chatting over coffee, as they take a break from shopping in the big stores on the avenue Victor Hugo.

Exchange "God, 10.1 plus commission!" The American girl complains to her friend as she checks the latest rates while behind the glass a dour woman runs her calculator to compute the transaction.

Preserved The visitors examine with close interest the coarse texture of a monk's habit preserved from the 17th century, which hangs beside a simple trestle couch, and study the collection of fetishistic relics of the Franciscan Order in the museum of the monastery at Cimiez.

Dusk Leaves of the aloe bushes return to a darker hue as dusk falls. On the far hillside a single light gleams from a villa in the neighbouring resort. On the right the tall pine leans away, its foliage spread against the evening sky. The clink of cutlery and children's voices are heard as families settle in for the night.

Translucent Translucent prawn skins lie discarded amongst sorrel and endive leaves, remains of the salad set beside a half finished bowl of fettucine pistou. "*Oui je mange un peu*", the mature blonde informs her husband at the bar, and smiles graciously at the waiter who prepares her beach mattress. She disrobes to a gold lame bikini to take some sun before lunch. The meal over the visitors walk around the coast to

Cap Ferrat, past shaded groves of olive trees and small inlets to private residences. In one bay a lean bald man with a hook nose exercises his alsatians, throwing heavy chain leashes into the sea for collection. Broad flat slabs of mottled stone appear under the surface of the water, which passes from pale green drifts in the shallows and out into the violet deep.

Poolside A tall skinny German jives by the poolside bar, a transistor held to his ear. A mother lies on a sun deck surrounded by her three topless daughters who glance hopefully around them for signs of attention."Une glace chocolat et vanille, et un citron avec framboise", the visitor requests. "*Pan, pan, pan*", goes the disco beat at the bar as the lean young man filles the glasses, laying a generous amount of lemon ice over the raspberry flavour. "C'est le grand scoop", says the visitor. "Oui, le grand scoop", he replies.

Silent The tall pine stretches silent against the evening sky. On a first floor balcony a mother hosts a gathering of adolescents who chatter endlessly about nothing in particular, excited by each other's company.

Numerals on a digital watch drop away second by second as the gathering of adolescents chatter endlessly, excited by each other's company.

Patterns Irregular shapes are printed in varied tints of ultramarine blue, green and yellow, bringing to mind the broken vertebrae of some fossilized creature, repeated in lively patterns over the drapes in the apartment.

Bronzed The woman turns and stretches. She kneels to adjust her narrow shoulder straps and smooths the costume tighter over her torso, flexing bronzed shoulders and thighs and shaking out her mane of thick glossy black curls.
Afternoon A bird twitters in the foliage of the tall pine. On an upper balcony a man in steel framed spectacles leans to inspect the body of a

woman who sunbathes in the clearing below. In a first floor apartment a maid operates a high powered hoover to clear the debris of departed guests.

Dutchman Sweat glistens on the torso of the powerfully built Dutchman who relaxes on a sun deck by the pool. He sits forward to extinguish a cigarette and finish his beer, adjusts his headphones and continues reading his book.

Helper A boy points out a possible sore on his thigh to the girl next to him, who leans over to inspect the troubled spot with solicitous interest.

Bar Belle A stately black model in brief day-glo pink costume drinks at the beach bar with her agent and minder. She stretches her legs, arching her back, and laughs. Her agent smiles but shoots a searching glance at the fattening young man who leers approvingly at her provocative change of pose.

Amused A woman with coiled red hair does a little dance to amuse her husband who continues reading on the balcony. Finding no response she straightens her white ribbed bikini and takes another chair, putting slippered feet up on the railings and lighting another cigarette.

Container The container folds and turns along sharp ridges, marked by deep indentations in its enamel surface. '*Mayo-Sieur*', parts of the brand name are truncated by the force of continuous use as the last drop is squeezed from the twisted remains of an exhausted tube of mayonnaise.

Reception A woman assists her husband in reading the map, picking places of interest and formulating a schedule of routes. The large dog by the door of the reception lounge yawns as rain continues to fall heavily outside.

By the Jetty Mist still covers the upper reaches of the hillside above the resort as the rain clears. Three young women stand by the low jetty, engaged in discussion and gazing at the water's edge.

On the Avenue The Moroccan who sits at the boulevard cafe table has a slight blemish above his left eye. He relaxes while the crowd swirls by in the avenue Jean Medecin in Nice. A thin woman in loose black tee shirt and slacks moves quickly for a bus, pressing forward through gangs of trippers with their stacked bags on the sidewalk. In a shop window shoes are arranged in rows of blue, brown, white, cream and grey, made in patent leather, suede and composition. A girl turns with mild interest through racks of lightweight jackets and skirts; pink, green, lemon and French blue. A couple pass; he, tanned with silver hair, in pale blue jeans and cream short sleeved shirt; she, plump-cheeked with bobbed hennaed hair, wearing black jacket, white trousers and sling-backed shoes. In the paved quarter vendeuses wait for custom, fanning themselves between racks of designer-label wares *Armand Thierry, Gaultier, Rykiel, Frizon*. Boys on scooters make short turns into the side streets to check the action, then switch around to speed back up the avenue.

Neighbours Strains of jazz filter from the TV set in the next apartment, entertaining the family at their evening meal. The gaunt father, seen earlier repairing a hair dryer, tries to control his boisterous children at the table. The excited commentary continues; shrieks, grunts, bangs, whistles and grotesque laughter emanate from the TV. "Et voila, messieurs-dames!" Applause for the clever tricks and the next act is introduced.

Cocktail The woman with coiled red hair, in a black silk top and light pantaloons, perches on the cocktail bar stool chatting with the young man who amuses her while he filters small cups of strong coffee.

Engaged While their children are engaged at the pool, the man and his wife take the opportunity to examine their holiday accounts.

Grecian A clump of palm trees shade the white residence by the railway line. Beyond, a Grecian style terracotta villa is glimpsed in the woods on the far hillside. In the early evening parents observe the smaller children as they play in and out of the pink flowered bushes that divide the gardens of the apartments. Two tall young women, both dark with long curled hair, in loose brown cotton skirts, come away from the tennis courts and smile at the scene. "Bon soir", they murmur as they pass.

Siesta A low breeze plays amidst the foliage of the tall pine and through the long leaved bushes that divide the gardens. The mechanical digger continues to drill at the rockface on the nearby construction site. In the apartment the woman lies on a blue divan while her children sleep in the late afternoon.

Part Four

Incident and a Memory

1988

Ratbag "You can't find them anywhere nowadays." "Find what?" "You know, those little packets, sherbet dabs." The girl attends to her client, plucking strands of fair hair through a tight-fitting rubber cap with long tweezers. Beside her pipes and fittings dangle from a chrome stand. The telephone rings and the dresser interrupts the haircut to go to the desk. "Shelley, your mum wants to speak to you." "What?" Says the girl. "*It's for you ratbag!*" He tells her.

The Street Two schoolgirls in purple jackets make faces at their friends in the bus before disappearing into the store. A woman exits through swing doors and gives her child a chocolate bar before pushing the buggy away. Further up the street an old man walks slowly, bent over and unsteady, supporting himself with two sticks while young girls zip by, laughing on rollerskates. Two men confer, kneeling by their bicycles parked against a tree. Behind them in an employment bureau women relax and chat casually, sitting amidst a scatter of files and papers on their desks, tired at the end of another day.

In Black A Chinese woman in a pink smock contemplates a small white panel, looking occasionally at the model who sits on a dais. She picks up some black on her brush and makes a broad mark for the back of his head. She pauses, then blocks in the bridge of his nose and hooded eyes with a bold stroke. Another defines the sharp jaw line. She lays down the brush and stands away from the easel to work out her next move.

Ad '88 A funfair train loops a spiral against the flaming colours of a setting sun. A carnival parade of comic characters makes its way along the broad avenue. A pretty girl flings open the shutters on a bright and sunny morning, scattering a flock of white doves. The chorus builds to a crescendo, recounting the benefits of a visit to the distant country.

The Candidate The candidate stands awkward on the steps of the Senate building. He smiles and waves to the forest of cameras which fences him in.

Switching Channels A woman recounts a tragic incident which affected her life, in a brave and composed manner before the steady gaze of the cameras. On another channel two fat girls jostle each other cheerfully to shrieks of laughter and encouraging shouts from the studio audience. The viewer goes to the kitchen to fill the sink with more dirty crockery ready to wash up and returns to watch an interesting report on social recovery from a major disaster, which contains useful, on the spot recordings of reactions of those caught up in the event, intercut with an update on the current state of affairs from the survivors. Then an elegant film of gipsy dancers from a poor district in Spain effectively evokes its haunting musical tradition as the man relaxes on the deep cushioned sofa at the end of the day.

Grill Bar The chicken casserole is set down on the red vinyl topped table. The man consumes a mouthful as a woman out shopping with her children occupies the opposite seats. A bone becomes lodged at the back of his throat. He swallows twice to check its presence and to try to shift it. Beads of sweat break out. The woman shoots a suspicious glance as she selects her children's menu. He looks down at the steaming plate of stew, then gets up to go outside and bring the entire contents up in the gutter. To his relief the obstacle is cleared and he returns to his seat to complete the meal with fruit salad and ice cream.

Discussion A well-presented young man sits to the right of the charming girl who chairs a discussion on the plight of the homeless. His views on the problem differ from those of the representative of the local area and they combat strategies and figures, becoming increasingly heated in their delivery. At the time signal the girl breaks in and closes the discussion, thanks the performers for their contribution and moves on to reveal the next topic of the evening.

Man A case is jammed between the sliding doors of the train to prevent their closing as a man forces his way into the carriage. He plants himself in a spare seat and elbows more space for his comfort. Aged about thirty five he wears a flat tweed cap, a straggly beard covers puffed cheeks. His small eyes are concealed by steel framed spectacles. He produces a cheese and onion roll from a bag and proceeds to munch his breakfast, breathing heavily between large mouthfuls. When completed his lips protrude and suck in, finding missing crumbs. He scratches his crotch and occasionally burps onion breath as he reads his literary supplement.

Victorian The young lady is prettily attired as a Victorian belle. She promotes a new London emporium open for summer tourists, thrusting leaflets in the hands of travellers as they rush from the train on their way to work.

Spilt At the end of the day the girl settles herself in the corner of the carrage, spreading an array of fruit beside her and on her lap. She unwraps a melon and digs away at the segment with a plastic spoon, smearing her cardigan with spilt juice in the process.

See Through A large man with silver hair and a red pitted face sits upright staring ahead, his hand gripping an unread paper. In the corner of the carriage a tired office worker slides downwards to the floor, his head thrown back and mouth open wide, seen through the large man's reflection in the glass.

Dazzled Soft white forms of deep sea creatures shiver and twitch, disturbed by harsh lights of the divers' probes. The waters froth and streams of bubbles rise while silvered fish tussle savagely, their teeth fastened on the wriggling victim. On another channel the famous performer executes at high speed a well rehearsed routine, exciting the many fans gathered in various venues on his world-wide tour. A continuous band dictates the list of his achievements and sales, as excerpts of his career flash before dazzled eyes.

Delete "Oh you must have one!" they chorus enthusiastically as one demonstrates the range of possibilities of the personal computer. "And here I can enter the name into the record and with this button delete. There! This person no longer exists, erazed completely and forever."The expert gleefully blanks the loved one from the screen.

Young Professional His strong boned face gains a waxed sheen in the greenish light, eyes unblinking behind large tortoiseshell spectacles. His light brown hair crinkles back in greased waves and the heavy tweed overcoat with upturned collar flaps open to show high waisted baggy trousers secured with a narrow belt. He leans back on the strap, head angled and mechanically chewing gum, and stares around at the other occupants in the carriage.

Twisting The woman props her face on her hands, pushing her spectacles off their perch. She twists and turns trying to find a comfortable position, pressed against the window of the carriage.

Subway Through the network of passages that connects the confused layout of Hammersmith Broadway, the low hum of a harmonium is heard somewhere in the dark subway. In a far cornera street musician stands philosophical, a dead cigarette dangling from his lip. He repeatedly presses two favourite chords on a small electric organ, his open suitcase ignored by the general passers by.

Black Girl Her hair is cut in a steep wedge above the slender neck, the flat top combed out sideways in rough strands. Her head turns slightly, showing a small gold ring with a long pendant that dangles from her ear. The knot of a narrow shoulder strap pushes up the collar of her soft leather jacket.

High Road A battered builder's van pushes over the crossing, impatient of confused pedestrians. A sharp wind gusts up the high road sending scudding leaves across the pavement. Late shoppers clutch their coats around them and make for the reassuring brightness of the large stores. "**Just get the fucking thing up!**" A small man in a trilby urges on his assistants as they fumble with the sign. "Come on love." The man at the fruit stall mutters narrow eyed, as a woman dithers over her purchase, a queue extending behind her. Crowds criss-cross on their various journeys; young mothers with loaded buggies zig-zag between commuters who rush to their station. "Can you tell me the time and where I can get a job?" A dishevelled man tries to catch their attention as they hurry past.

Insulted "He nearly had a heart attack when I told him, just slumped right off the bed to the floor." A girl with long chestnut hair laughs as she tells her companion. "and the things he said to me, I was so insulted!" 'Maybe he felt insulted too." Suggests the man. "But he said I'd lied to him." She pouts. "And had you?..There you are then." "But why should he be so horrible to me ?" The girl discusses her previous lover with her her new companion.

Slamming Doors A mature woman in a chain linked cloak and fur hat slams the door to the waiting room as she strides in. Then changing her mind she turns on her heel and stamps out, slamming the door again on her exit.

Allotment A bent metal spike dangles from a slack wire fence by the railway track. Thin smoke curls over patches of cabbage leaves and empty bean frames. An old man gathers his implements together in a barrow and moves slowly towards his small wooden shed. The stretch of open ground of the allotment is seen against a darkening skyline of office blocks, warehouses and low terraced cottages with bending red-tiled roofs.

Search The amiable beat of a country and western favourite replaces the solemn clank of mystic bells and scratched sounds of an experimental music programme. A narrow strip of orange light blinks and indicator numbers drop away in hundreds as the automatic tuner tracks through the babble of many commentators. The listener settles for a moment on the well-loved country series, changing to an animated discussion by sports experts which is quickly discarded in favour of a play on the passions of women. The dial moves among the fuzz and crackle of distant stations. The mode alters from radio to tape and the search is on for some classical entertainment from the extensive collection.

Walking A blind man taps his stick left and right, head raised staring ahead, as he makes his way steadily along the darkened street. Three young girls in white coats gather around the till in the chemist's shop to gossip at the end of the day. In the next window a bright array of leather goods; open wallets containing neat sets of scissors, combs, nail files and clippers. brogues, gloves, cases. A fine saddle set beside a shooting stick draped with a heavy tweed cape. Ahead the looming shape of a short man in a long raincoat carrying a full black shoulder bag. "Got the time please?"A youth in a tee shirt and pale slacks accosts him. The man obliges and presses on rapidly to the security of the riverside inn. Bells tinkle on boats moored by the bridge, small lights glint on the water's edge as a line of silhouetted figures make their way back to a neighbouring hamlet.

Wall The hand traces along the texture of an old brick wall that curves around by the lane leading to Richmond Park.

Alley Twisted metal springs of a buckled bed frame that stands beside a stack of empty cartons. A scatter of tin cans and papers overflows from split garbage bags in the space of a small yard at the end of a side alley, the narrow access to the back of buildings on the high street, located between a second hand furniture store and an electrical repair shop.

Evening The quizmaster beams at a row of eager young contestants and relaxes them with some playful questions, complimenting them on their display of cuddly toy mascots. Tyres of a passing car cast up the rainy surface of the road. A rhinoceros yawns, revealing rows of yellowing pegs set in a cavernous jaw, as a plate of toasted cheese is deposited on the sofa for consumption. A tall girl glides elegantly from a limousine, assisted by her handsome chauffeur, then floats up the broad curved stairway of a palatial interior. A golden bottle of perfume appears for a moment, then dissolves in a dreamy mist. The mouth chews on a morsel of bread as we pass over hilly landscapes with winding blue rivers while the voice-over tells of disappearing trees in a distant country. A low spreading hum marks the track of an incoming flight.

Incident and a Memory Cameras probe the wreckage searching for sight of any injured or dead amidst the twisted metal. In an old movie a girl escorts her gallant soldier, leaving to join his regiment at the front. Light focuses on her beautiful grave face as she drifts into the distance, a small figure lost in the lengthening shadows on the broad platform.

Memory and an Incident The older woman sits beside the beautiful young girl to convey the dreaded news from the battlefield. Harsh lights flood the hospital ward to assist the recording, as an important visitor comforts the injured while doctors advise reporters on the progress of recovery.

The Leader A man affectionately touches the arm of the leader who presents him with an emblem of recognition for his services. In a furrowed field the leader stands and surveys the scorched earth, while teams of helpers pick through the scattered debris.

Seasonal Silken bands unwrap and float apart, releasing the lid of the box to reveal alluring rows of dark chocolates. The contents rise up from their tray and disperse in a sparkling mist. A tall white candle flickers by a spray of holly, setting the backdrop to the seasonal gift.

Entertainers Two pairs of empty spectacles are suspended against a bright pink background, framed by a bow of pretty striped ribbon.

Parked Car Nightlights catch the dull sheen of a metallic blue saloon, casting a gleam along the silvered strip on the side of the car that stands alone in the private car park of the business centre. The car with a heavy bowed roof rack resembles a squat insect, waiting to jump. A girl leans on the opened door of her double parked red sports model chatting casually to a young man on the kerb, her headlights full on and warning light flashing the cars behind, as they try to negotiate the narrow passage round the obstruction.

Diagonal The handsome young director creates an elegant and assured impression on a panel of national representatives as he details reasons for his company's acceptance of the significant contract. An illustration appears of the intended site of operations, the long grey block of an empty factory cutting a low diagonal across the screen, a sheen of drizzle dampening the forecourt.

Sign "I shall be working in the period between Christmas and the New Year, I find it is an ideal time to concentrate one's efforts and I expect to achieve a great deal. "The thin man smiles with satisfaction at his statement to his colleague. "It was twenty minutes before they displayed a sign informing us that the six-twenty had been cancelled." His fellow traveller eventually responds, staring glumly through the window as the train waits on the tracks for a change of signal.

Dark Window "I make frequent use of my local library, in a way as a return on my rates." The man converses with a woman returning from a shopping trip in town. "I am also the proud owner of a fine collection of books which provide a constant source of pleasure. "My daughter is an artist and is also employed as an attendant in a cemetary, so I knew she would relish this volume by Edgar Allan Poe." The woman shows one of her purchases to the man whose profile divides in two, reflected in different levels of the dark window in the carriage.

Drunk A drunk claps his hands and barks like a dog before hiding his face and coughing repeatedly. Pigeons strut about his feet in the green nightlights, pecking for scraps among scattered papers. '*Homeless and Hungry*'. The message is scrawled on a piece of board hung round the young man's neck. He sits cross legged, puffy faced and moaning on the first landing of the station steps, ignored in the rush of passers by.

Mad ***"Oh God! Fucking Hell!"*** The woman's jaw slackens and her eyes roll as she grips the metal handle of her seat. She presses the side of her head, impatient at the slow movement of the traffic. Her neighbour smiles at her benignly, observing her emotional state. "***Excuse me!***" The woman shouts at two bewildered schoolboys, forcing her way from the bus at the next stop.

Pure "They think they have the weapons to deal with us, but I can assure you that just one of our submarines could wipe out the lot of them in seconds." A vagrant converses with amiable passengers on the nature of global conflict. "What we need is a figurehead, a leader pure and clear that the people will respect." He continues, "Would any of you have 20p to get me through the barrier?" He asks at the end stop. The travellers laugh and leave him alone in the carriage.

By the Bridge A man points his camera in the direction of a cluster of small cottages which overlook the bend in the river near Twickenham. A raised walkway gives access to moored boats and rusting barges, some awaiting repair in the corrugated building above the bank. Gulls screech and wheel about over the water. A heavily built man in a maroon quilted jacket and cream trousers poses his aged mother beside the railings for another snapshot while a boy parks his bike and stretches out on a bench, discarding the wrapper of his fruit bar. A man sits in his car with the windows tight shut, consuming alternate mouthfuls of chips and a burger. He stares fixedly ahead as groups of visitors wander about by the arched bridge to the island and along different levels of steps which lead to the water's edge.

Paint Marking Heavy white paint crumbles in parts to reveal dark grey tarmac, a corroded strip marking divisions of space in the small car park. A bright coloured stain spreads over the pavement and down the kerb into the gutter. Blue footprints trail away from the evidence of a dropped can of paint.

Double Order "One apple fritter, one Big Mac, two coffees." A couple make their selection and await service while the next customer takes their place in the queue."Two cheeseburgers, one quarter pounder, three regular fries, one coffee, one chocolate shake, one small orange." The girl rushes to and fro between the drinks dispenser and chip tray. "There you are sir, two cheeseburgers and one apple fritter.." The man's eyes roll upwards and his companion purses her lips. "Perhaps I should repeat my request?" He enquires. The girl becomes increasingly harassed and confused as bags pile up on the counter. "If they don't deliver your order in one minute it's free." A second man jokes with the first.

Blackened Striplights gleam in the early evening, reflecting on several levels of the large office development. In a side street a stocky man in a large blue parka lugs full plastic bags towards his car. Up the brick walls of a disused factory unit a tangle of sprayed messages and personalised signatures crowd for attention. A bar of blackened wood is dislodged from the framework of one of several derelict garages, set beyond the bright shopping arcade.

Walking Man Powerful build, short greasy hair combed forward over a low brow. Hooded eyes with a determined expression on a broad face, full lipped with slack jowls. The man in a loose black track suit and short nylon jacket strides purposefully towards the built up zone from the park after his ritual exercise.Nervous, bespectacled with curled hair,lean frame, slope-shouldered, the young man keeps close to the side, moving slowly with frequent pauses to examine the special offers on display in the store windows. Dark blue suit, long overcoat casually draped over the left arm, he walks briskly away from the station. A lock of straight black hair falls over arched eyebrows. A sallow complexion and sharp features register a sharp and quizzical expression as he passes in the darkened street.

Part Five

Holiday Island

Sardinia 15.07. - 29.07.89

Sunlight A pair of sunglasses stands against an open bag of crisps and beside a jar of face cream.

Shadows Feet rest on pale green sheets next to a discarded pink tee shirt. Sunlight flickers on the open wardrobe door as the child sits on the bed, cutting intriguing shapes from sheets of coloured paper. Feet rest on pale green sheets next to a discarded pink tee shirt. Twilight casts long shadows from net curtains onto the wardrobe and from an open door onto the plastered wall.

Hotel An immaculately groomed hotel clerk obliges with a currency exchange, finely manicured fingers flicking through the notes, then withdraws to the cool white office beyond the pot plants, as the visitor departs. The hotel pool remains empty in the intense heat of mid-day, shutters are closed on the apartments.

Main Route Large coils of black tubing stand in the open area by the sports ground. Three men toss parts of metal fencing onto the back of their truck, and stack materials ready for the new construction. At the rear of an empty villa workers gather in the shade to pass a bottle of wine. Beyond the petrol station on the main route into the hills, a flash of sunlight catches the roof of a car, proceeding in the far distance.

Cream and Sweat White sun cream mingles with droplets of perspiration that spread over folds of pale flesh, and continues carelessly smeared on to boldly patterned shorts. Perspiration and cream mingle in the folds of pale flesh, compressed by the tight garter belt of the woman's brief costume.

Still Life with an Ant A long sharp knife rests across an open pack of salami that conceals a half eaten segment of melon, its pips spilt over bread rolls that nestle in a deep white plate. An ant crawls hopefully up the side of the round table, to be brushed aside by a descending fork.

Floating A young boy attends to his fishing rod, preparing bait for his line on the jetty wall. In the water a large man with a snorkel steers in varied directions, searching for prey with his spear gun. A bronzed fair-haired youth in bright pink shorts steadies himself on a lilo which drifts with the current caused by a passing dinghy.

Galmarket A broken bottle top is kicked aside into stacks of cartons, discarded beside the walkway to the Galmarket. A helpful assistant directs the visitor to the trolley ramp and indicate the location of cereals at the rear of the store. A queue forms at the butcher's counter where a whole dead pig is displayed under glass alongside fat coils of salami and rounds of cheese.

Evening Past tumbled heaps of masonry, glass fragments and sundry refuse scattered over the burnt earth banks by the main route, to the top of the open ground and entrance to the villas. Down the long avenue leading to the bay a brunette in bright red shorts gestures to her companion in a sports car before opening the door to load their beach gear. A man walks by carrying a full black bag towards the disposal point. A woman in striped slacks carefully sweeps her front step, while a mature couple salute their friends' departure, exchanging greetings in French and Italian. Round globe lights amidst the azaleas and bougainvilleas mark the way along narrow paths to the villa door.

On Parade A ginger haired woman in a brief top and candy stripe shorts sucks a vanilla cone as she walks ahead of her escort, a watchful young man in pleated cream slacks and steel-rimmed spectacles. Two ladies pass by the table, one in an ultra slim white crochet dress, the other in a tropical print sarong. They circle the cafe bar for attention and move on to the adjacent restaurant. The waiter brings impressive glasses of vanilla and chocolate ice, which quickly dissolve into deep brown pools.

Interior On the window sill a box of Kellog's Corn Flakes, a jar of Nescafe '*Classic Blend*', '*Last*' detergent, Lipton's '*Yellow Label*' tea bags, and below, several black disposal bags in a *Parmelat* carton. A white towel is casually draped over the chair set at a square dining table, over which hangs a brooding winter landscape by '*Marc*'. Creams and powders line the glass fronted cabinet, a bottle of cologne stands beside a charming arrangement of artificial flowers in a fluted vase, there to welcome new visitors to the residence. A broom leans against the glass fronted cabinet in which is seen the reflection of a child asleep on a divan.

Beach Red and black sandals and skooba gear in a yellow plastic basket, left by a beached dinghy with outboard motor.

A young couple bat a small red ball to and fro with practised expertise. A mature Italian woman carefully picks hairs from her legs with tweezers while her children splash about at the water's edge.

Red Sun The woman sweeps her terrace and arranges towels to dry on a stand. Conversation drifts from a family in a nearby villa as a red sun descends behind blue mountains.

Old and Young An elderly couple gingerly feel their way out into the deep and make steady headway towards a prominent rock. By the jetty a young girl switches a mane of dark curled hair over her shoulder and stretches upright. She stands poised at the water's edge. The light catches her thigh as she points an elegant toe in the sand, turning slightly to regard thc divers from the headland. The features descend in deep drawn lines to a small chin and hollowed neck. Wrinkled flesh sags bulging in a bright green costumc. A broad brimmed black straw hat protects her from the glare of midday. She puts aside her book to peer over half framed spectacles at the small children, who splash about in the shallows.

Hunter Three small silver fishes wriggle on the fork of a harpoon spear as the man proudly demonstrates his success to a group of admiring children.

Pink Wall An irregular faded pink wall separates one area of scrub and undergrowth from another. Low stone walls support three levels of terraces with neatly tiled paths leading up to each apartment. Sunlight filters through tall trees which sway in a low breeze. Families chatter and play in the water as evening draws in over the bay.

The Listener "A lecturer in finance", the woman from a neighbouring apartment juts her jaw with determination as she names her profession, and describes the exploits of her family in their active ventures over the island. Impressed by her energy the listener retires to the quiet of the villa to recline in another extended siesta.

White Chairs White chairs form a triangle by the round table on the terrace, scattered with coloured papers from the child's activity. Bottles of sun cream, mats, spades and costumes fill a large soft bag at the side, which awaits the next journey to the beach.

Orange and Pink The boy drops orange flippers in the water and returns to his mat, then runs back to fall forward in the sea with a splash. On the rocks above a mature bronzed couple contemplate the scene, elegant in bright orange and pink costumes. A young girl in black and magenta stripes kneels prettily to enquire the comfort of her aged relative, who nestles in the shade of a beach umbrella.

Englishman Fellow compatriots with their wives greet each other at the beachside restaurant and settle at adjacent tables to study the menu. A young waitress awaits their signal and approaches with words of welcome to take their order. The tall Englishman sits straight backed, passing an odd word in low tones with his wife who bends foward nervously over her plate. His steak arrives which he accepts without acknowledgement. He carefully sections the meat into triangles, working from the left, and proceeds to deposit each part in order of cutting in his mouth, chewing methodically as he assesses the quality of the meal.

À Deux The young couple is seated at a charmingly decorated table à deux near the sands. She looks fondly down at the little ones at play nearby, while he hunches over his portion of pasta, quickly sucking up the strands in order to avoid spillage from the bowl.

Daughters The pushy father proudly parades his voluptuous daughters on the beach, gaining admiration from other men and guarded looks from their wives. He noisily installs a parasol while the young women comb their hair and smooth their weighty thighs. His imposing wife suddenly settles in a deck chair, which nearly collapses under the impact.

Ferry Crowds of tourists pour off the ferry returning from the islands. A tall blonde in crinkled check mini-shorts hangs onto her beau, finding her way amidst the jostling throng. Kids lounge with blaring radios, surveying the beach from parapet railings. A fat man in a giant sombrero and pink Bermudas pulls a giant lilo with an inflated plastic palm tree up to the waterline.

Interior in Pink and Blue Pink sunlight casts blue shadows from the French windows onto the corner of the room. Artificial flowers on a glass cabinet are seen again in the tall mirror, beside doors to the terrace.

Chain Link Patterns of luminous pale yellow play on the sediment and swirl in areas of seaweed and coral. Bathers move cautiously into the drifting current, looking down at shoals of small fishes which scatter in their path."I have never seen such large fishes gathered in one place." The heavily built man lifts his snorkel to report to his wife from the water, before reversing flippers up, with a spray of his snorkel, to return to the deep.

Carton Broken plastic tape partially obscures the bold red design of an empty *San Carlo Patatine* ***'Rustiche'*** forty stock crisps carton, that sits behind a metal framed deck chair, and before a brilliant gleam of white light on the soft edged plaster wall seat that borders the terrace.

Young Italians A girl reclines offering herself to the sun, floating on a lilo far out in the violet deep. The heavily built man prepares his mask and snorkel for another expedition. On the beach a woman chats with her companions, alternately sucking a bright green ice and drawing on a cigarette. A local trader hawks garish costumes and jewellery amongst the beach parties. To the right a gathering of elders conducts a discreet conversation under the olive trees. Two young Italians lie side by side, lithe and bronzed in black swim wear, decorated with fine gold chains. A pair of flippers are left leaning together upended in the sand, a small sculpture in the scene.

Shutters Jointed slats are reinforced with crossbars and diagonal struts, finished with strong steel bolts and hinges. The shutters are hooked back to the wall at an acute angle to the open French windows, the ensemble completed in a rich deep brown varnish. Straight backed chairs are drawn up to the square dining table. Right-angled bars of wood form the legs, secured with countersunk brass discs.

Shower Accumulations of pale green corrosion line the outlet to the shower tray. A pair of textured plastic screens hang loose from the track on a projecting aluminium frame.

Cars A pert blonde disrobes to reveal a bright yellow costume, decorated on the rear with pretty frills and a risque black bow. Above her on the headland, cars are parked in closed ranks, vying for the nearest access to the beach.

The Deep Along the jetty the pink surface gives way to layers of silver and ochre granite, glittering with fragments of glass and amber. Below the waterline the crumbling blocks turn red brown with black markings, covered in parts with soft patches of weed. Moon-like reflections of discarded can lids appear on the floor of the bottle green deep.

Checking Seated on a wall above the beachside restaurant, a youth flicks rapidly through a stranger's wallet, checking the cash while glancing disinterested at the family photos, before slotting it into his back pocket. A young girl pauses to check her hair and fall of her dress before setting off for the village square from a block of apartments. A woman drapes her arms around her companion's neck and entwines him in a close embrace, promising significant developments in their evening together, while he looks furtively over her shoulder for casual spectators.

Columns Mortar is roughly scraped between the blocks of cream stone, pitted with ochre and black markings. Various shapes and sizes are fitted together with ingenuity to make substantial square columns, that support the crossbeams on the roof of the terrace.

Roadside Tangled strips of brown adhesive tape; floating lengths of bleached polythene wrapping; dumped containers, cartons, bottles; scraps of tissue, butt ends, plastic, wire, broken glass and a flattened '*Tomate*' can, amidst the pink shale, grit, dried gorse and heather on banks beside the main route, that runs past the local shopping precinct.

Checkout "Latte fresco?" The visitor enquires of the girl at the checkout, who signals a negative as she totals the bill. "*Latte, latte*", the queue takes up the request, pointing to empty shelves.

Amber Sun The child throws a ball to its mother on the terrace as an amber sun descends behind blue mountains.

Red and Blue 'Ignienica Top', gay red and blue bands decorate the protective film, the diagonal lines following folds and creases in the polythene wrapping. The cover is torn open at the bars of the product code, the number sequence **8.07825.00** leads incomplete to the edge of the plastic. The pure white cylindrical form of a fresh roll of '*Marbo*' tissue is revealed, placed on rich blue ceramic tiles, below the sweeping oval rim of the bidet.

Walkway A covered walkway leads the visitor past elegant showcases of leading designers; *Gianfranco Ferre, Gianni Vercace, Stefanel, Sonia Rykiel, Gold Line, Christian Lacroix, Armani.* Window shoppers pause as they drift along the piazzas, checking price tags and peer through glass doors into cool interior where the occasional client relaxes in a padded armchair.

Tempting An amusing silver plate lobster; a bouquet of flowers carved in rose quartz; miniature gold dice in a presentation box; a shimmering rainbow sequinned hand bag; a stand of mirrored sunglasses; a revealing black chiffon cocktail dress with embroidered silk petals; an inventive combination of multi-coloured deco-patterned shirt, with a wool jacket and high waisted leather trousers by *Versace*; cream panama hat with floral band, matching shoes and bag by *Gucci*; little faces on mosaic pendants in a jeweller's window; a glass table supported by twisting carved dragons, and nearby a decorative blue glass service, all tempting the eye of the spectator.

On-Line The counter clerk enters the passport details into his computer and scans the information that flows from the printer. Details of the visitor's place of residence and movement on the island are confirmed, before being placed on-line for completion of the exchange.

Square A policeman in a shaded corner carefully surveys the empty square in the village centre before cautiously moving into the sunlight, murmuring observations into his two way receiver.

Handyman A two handed saw, machete, drill and chisel, lie by the work bench in front of an unoccupied apartment. The stoop-shouldered handyman supervises a garden hose as sprinklers play over the lawns and flowerbeds. Tall trees sway in a gentle breeze, with brilliant sunlight filtering to the terrace of the apartment. Tapping sounds come from the gardens as the handyman continues his schedule of repairs. Tall trees sway in a gentle breeze, silhouetted against blue puffs of cloud covering an orange sunset. The stars of *The Plough* appear in the darkening sky.

Diners The popular restaurant quickly fills, with families well dressed for a social evening. Two young men see their girls arrive and run to the car park to escort them inside, then stand nervously surveying the interior for a suitable table. A grim faced bullish man circles the buffet loading his plate from the many dishes. Outside, at the rear of the establishment, a lone cow philosophically munches in a field of scrub.

Study A charming study of blue waves, fresh summer sky and a rocky headland by *Felice Castelli* decorates the dining room of the apartment, the plaster walls of which are marked in places with the remains of rapidly dispatched insects.

Beach A young man lays his companion down at the water's edge and arranges her comely legs in the shale and grit of the beach, pushing her face to one side before stepping back to make his photographic study. The proud father studies his two daughters as they bat a pink ball to and fro in the waves, occasionally intervening to give them further instruction in the game. Neat rows of bamboo canes are secured with wire ties slotted between corrugated plastic sheets and supporting timbers of the veranda sun roof. Beyond the terrace tall trees sway in the heat of mid afternoon. A child eats a tomato at a round table, climbing down from its chair from time to time to study the movement of a brown bug, that slowly traverses the red tiled floor.

Sounds Spattering of water from a garden hose over the flowering bushes by the apartment; the hum of a distant power boat; shuffling chairs and grunts from the occupants in the upper storey of the villa.

Window Pale green bedcover entangled with a white towel and grey striped pyjamas, casually draped over the back of a chair. A boy and girl returning from the beach look quickly through an open window in the apartment. On the terrace two children lean on the round table as their mother supervises their drawings.

Gourmets A magnificent lobster is set on a trolley beside the table to be inspected by the eager gourmets. The creature twitches its claws and raises its proboscis, becoming aware of its imminent fate. The diners arrange their seating, the men pushing back their chairs for ample accommodation while the ladies converse before the meal, relaxing with a cigarette. Several waiters with the maitre d' bring the prepared trolley

Part Six

CLOUDS and SUNS

1989

Standing Woman 1-3 Sunlight catches the flap of the pointed shoe, the pale material of loose cut trousers folding in shallow creases at the hem. A broad belt hangs unbuckled from loops on the long back coat. Two full soft leather bags are casually slung from her shoulders, the collar turned up to shield her neck. She stands straight with one foot forward, head turned away, light brown hair drawn tightly back and secured with a red ribbon. She relaxes, flipping at random through pages of a popular magazine, long strands of fair hair spread over the back of a checked cashmere jacket, her head pressed against the glass partition of the carriage. A heavy cloak is draped with dramatic effect over a long green skirt, worn with sturdy brown boots. The winter outfit is enhanced by a round felt hat set firm on curled hair over bespectacled features. She strides into the carriage and takes her place in the centre aisle, glaring ferociously at seated fellow passengers.

Beside the Track Rotting sleepers are stacked in sets of three, half buried by piles of crushed and blackened leaves. Thin wire winds round some broken metal railings that lean over at the head of the bank. Sundry refuse and discarded belongings scatter amongst overgrown bushes and a tangled web of branches. A high bridge leads over to sets of playing fields and an industrial site. Lines of poplars fade into the low mist. Behind a small shed lie forgotten bags of shale, breeze blocks, paint cans and tools left from repairs, beside the track which leads between suburban stations.

Provisions 1-4 Through gleaming metal slats can be seen an impressive mound of assorted purchases an '*Airwick*' freshener nestles amidst rolls of soft pink tissue, exotic tins of Italian sauce and cellophane packets of part-baked baguettes, plastic tubs of high grade margarine, a mini-selection of cheeses, many flavoured yoghurts, cling-wrapped vegetables, choice cuts of bloodied meat and, rising above the pile, an imposing, economy-size bag of dog meal. A hand reaches down to clear the goods onto the checkout. As the basket empties, the cheerful floral print of a woman's pretty summer skirt appears through the bars of the trolley.

"*Orange Soda, one litre?*" The assistant requests a price on her call-phone. The mature couple frantically sort through their trolley as she makes rapid additions and shuffles items on the moving band to the back of the counter. The man hastily retrieves a twelve-pack of lagers to load first into the box.

A tray of gourmet cat food breaks open and little cartons scatter into the heap of provisions that await accounting.

"Four 'Steakhouse Original Beefburgers with Onion' ?" The assistant requests a price on her call-phone.She accounts a cling-wrapped roll of pork, digestive biscuits, '*McCann's Oven Chips*', lamb chops, cereal, instant coffee, dog food, crisps, lagers, two litre milk container, jam, mayonnaise, spiced buns, quick-cook spaghetti, '*Heinz*' soup, dairy cream sponge, peeled plum tomatoes, mini-cheese selection, '*Twix*', '*Mars Bars*', frozen pizza. The man completes his credit card transaction and joins his wife at the end of the moving band to help load their provisions. "Fresh chicken, £3.05; frozen green beans, 79p; '*Premier*' orange juice, £1.59p." The assistant pauses to stare vacantly at the lengthening queue as she loses track. The customer taps a pen on the counter, impatient for the girl to resume her addition.

Man and Car

Ignition The man approaches his car and with a smooth swivel movement from the right hip, inserts his ignition key to unlock the door.

Grip The man rests his sweating face on the back of his hands that grip the bar of his steering wheel. He remains motionless, slumped sideways in the parked car at the rear of the superstore.

Stopped The man tenses and signals sharply to the hesitant driver in front, repeatedly sounding his horn to press on the stopped car at the junction.

Tea Garden The man puts down the tray and seats himself, confidently placing his right foot on the woman's chair and lighting a cigarette. He leans forward to engage her in conversation while she examines the cake and places some in her mouth, staring ahead and chewing, in profile, in the tea garden.

The man leans forward, addressing the girl in an animated fashion. She turns and looks at him steadily and continues chewing.

The girl with dark brown hair, tied with a red ribbon, chews silently as she regards the man who leans towards her, smoking a cigarette and chatting, in the tea garden.

Children run in and out of the ornamental flower beds and chase the pigeons as a girl raises a slice of cake to her mouth and closes her eyes, enjoying the soft light of a late winter afternoon in the tea garden.

Children rattle the metal signs to the cafeteria and chase the pigeons as a woman raises a slice of cake to her mouth and closes her eyes, enjoying the soft light of a late winter afternoon in the tea garden.

Flashes Cheerful flashes of bright designs play with images of native life in the informative guide to a distant country.

A young doctor gently examines an unwell cat as a local woman looks on, concerned for its well-being.

Powerful searchlights beam on the plane that arrives on the runway, carrying the leader on his mission. A reception committee of the country's dignitaries await his arrival with due ceremony on the tarmac.

A young man and his girl sit in the corner of the bar, engaged in humorous banter. After a few moments they are joined by another companion who informs them of a new development in his life. The couple laugh and embrace, and the light turns turquoise blue in the girl's glass of bitter lemon.

Little fishes fizz and sizzle in the pan as a travelling gourmet demonstrates his culinary skills to a gathered audience of master chefs in a neighbouring country. They sample the results and compliment him in their own language as he makes discreet asides to the camera for the benefit of people watching him at home. The master chefs present a travelling gourmet with their prize medal and inscribed commendation which he accepts while making discreet asides to the camera during the ceremony, for the benefit of people watching him at home.

Office Radios 1-3 Raucous sounds of a music hall cabaret on one channel cut across a girl's nervous chattering about her life and work on another, her continous monologue steadied with soft encouragement by the experienced presenter.

The presenter makes a concise and informative introduction to the next guest who launches into a detailed description of her medical history, interrupted occasionally by a doctor's contributed assessment. A young girl chatters to her friends in the office as her printer rattles off streams of text. A cackle of laughter bursts from the radio and cuts across a woman's emotional account of her suffering, prompted with gentle encouragement by the experienced presenter.

Evening - Four Frames Brilliant sunlight catches the leading edge of the fighter's wing as it speeds above the clouds. It turns through an acute angle, the movement captured in four stop frames, enhanced by the rising sensual chant of girls' voices in a background pop song.

Submarine The sinister black shape of a submarine rises above the surface carrying its cargo of ultimate destruction. Below decks the loyal crew recount their beliefs and discipline while a roving camera indicates a varied menu being prepared for consumption aboard the vessel.

The Detective The detective casts a sympathetic glance at the elegant young woman as he informs her of a tragic incident. Harsh lights flatten her skin tone to a smooth beige, her fine-boned features modelled with strong black shadows that continue to her white roll neck pullover. The detective's craggy jaw accords with a world weary expression in his eyes as he stirs his coffee, awaiting her reaction.

Clouds and Suns The detective sits with the elegant girl in the bar, silent as he awaits her reaction to the tragic incident. By a large spotlit pool the detective doggedly pursues a solution to the mysterious death of a young woman. In lowered tones a newsgirl relates the recent demise of a soap star, with extracts re-run from key performances. A cheerful commentator follows with a sports update. The acid orange of the weather girl's dress vibrates against brilliant emerald green of the wall chart, as she points to a pleasing arrangement of little clouds and suns.

Beside the Bridge A small dog cocks its leg against the railings and proceeds along the towpath. A girl comes slowly down the steps while a cyclist awaits her exit with his bike on the ramp. On a moored boat a woman tugs the hem of her mini-shorts while the gentlemen engage in concentrated conversation over coffee. A man in dark glasses stands motionless on the bridge, looking down at the eddying current.

Beer Garden The man laughs broadly at the girl's remark and leers as she exits towards the Ladies, sunlight shimmering through her cotton skirt. "Kevin, get down from that slide !" A woman shouts and clips the screaming child as she collects him back.

Crossing A balding, mature man in a dark suit measures his steps with great care, placing one foot before the other on the painted bars as he moves in a straight line over the crossing.

Ghost The mature man in the corner furtively lowers his paper to regard a young girl who relaxes with her feet up in an adjacent seat, her casual black jacket with silver buttons open, white silk blouse loosened in the close heat. She slips sideways dozing, strands of fair hair spread over slackened shoulders, alluring tanned calves revealed in tight pink breeches. Beyond, a lean bespectacled youth sits upright, staring ahead. His ghost overlays the sleeping girl, reflected in the pale blue glass, his image exactly imposed on a vacant seat in the carriage.

Riverside A girl squats behind a bush, dress hitched up, and chats to her companion. A mature couple roll over in the grass, locked in a passionate embrace. Further along a crumpled individual scowls isolated from the verge. Thick green sediment blocks the water's surface, with sundry garbage drifting up to the riverbank. An empty plastic Coke bottle floats away in the main current. Two men sit on a bench and stare at the water while a boat packed with trippers backs into the mainstream to begin its tour. Young crews hoist their long boats from stands and slip them into the water. They take their places and await further orders from their leader. The girls watch from the side, chattering gaily to each other, excited by the competition and their team's physique and prowess.

Sandwich Bar "Look at them standing there, no money." The woman behind the counter points to the group of men by the door of the sandwich bar. "It's true - I'm skint, he's skint, you're skint," one replies.

"Well, what do you want then ?" The woman asks. "Teas two". "Teas two, what ?" "Teas two, two sugars," they chuckle knowingly.

Mulberries "They make the most delicious fruit pies," the woman informs the Welshman who watches her pluck mulberries from the broad foliage of the grand old tree, "but one must take care in the picking - look at the stains." She thrusts out a gory red hand at him, dripping with juice. Beyond the beer garden, on the island, a party relaxes with drinks in the pleasant shade of the yacht club.
"They have no objection to your collecting the fruit from this tree," the woman refers to the landlords of the establishment, "indeed, they positively encourage it. Bilberries must be the similar fruit in Wales ?" The visitor agrees, watching her activity. "But there, I've spotted my blouse." The woman remarks, aggravated.

Domestic The hourly transmission conveys the order of significant events: accidents, disputes, international trade figures. The items cross with the woman's voice as she discusses possible menus for forthcoming meals. Familiar voices act out the developing saga of the well-loved country series. The woman is silent, concentrated on the unfolding drama as she prepares the table.

Clearing The man kneels on his forecourt and with a short-bladed knife carefully clears spare earth which shows up between cracks in the paving stones.

Tapping The man taps the window frame at regular intervals, checking for an even drop of the sash as he adjusts the balance of the mechanism.

Bubbling Cheerful clashing of cymbals and drums with squeaking pipes introduce an imminent report of a journey in Mexico a woman describes the trials and discoveries of her family's recent boating adventure, specialists explain the system of food quality controls, voices are raised in lively political debate, and a panel of experts advises on seasonal gardening problems. Extracts from the schedule of morning programmes attract attention as a wooden spoon slowly stirs a small pan of bubbling baked beans.

Drain Browning dead leaves curl round the metal bars of an old arched drain set into the muddy bank below a narrow pathway which leads to the riverside.

Lustrous A soft amber light glows through fine lace curtains, revealing a precise arrangement of small square framed pictures detailed flower studies, dreamy landscapes, charming wildlife miniatures. Fitted rows of mahogany shelves display a fine collection of ornate porcelain vases set in order of size to the largest in the centre, lustrous in deep plum and cream glaze, that takes pride of place in the comfortably furnished front room of the ground floor flat.

Retail "I am waiting !" A gaunt, unshaven man shouts at his neighbour as the queue builds up at the cash desk. "99p." The assistant hands a receipt to the customer and fumbles with a plastic bag for the purchase.

Opening In the bar a fattish man in white shirtsleeves leans against the wall sweating and laughs as he raises a wine glass to his lips. In a darkened room of the exhibition, businessmen gather in close groups to discuss matters of importance in lowered voices. In the heat of the crowded room an attractively arranged dish of pate turns a deeper shade of pink. Cream vol-au-vents yellow and portions of cheese curl on their biscuits under the glare of little spotlights.

Artists "Are you quite well ?"The helpful assistant enquires of the visitor who sweats visibly in the close and stuffy atmosphere, pausing to grip the table as they turn through several albums of artists. "Oh they really enjoy to buy companies over here." The lean, bespectacled assistant converses with a heavily built American - tanned, in a light grey suit. Beyond the glass doors to the gallery a merry throng of office workers gathers outside a public house to enjoy a lunchtime drink. The visitor regards the large canvases in the cool white space. Beyond the glass doors a merry throng of office workers gathers outside a public house to enjoy a lunchtime drink. In the street the visitor passes a final word with the gallery assistant near the merry throng of office workers gathered outside a public house. Beyond, large canvases can be glimpsed through glass doors to the cool white space.

Dot "And what do we do now, Dot ?" The reassuring voice of the controller guides the young woman in a clown's costume around brightly patterned screens and boxes in the studio. She completes some simple tasks for the information of the children who watch the recorded presentation enrapt, enjoying her competent performance on a variety of instruments.

Patch A girl in a cheerful, multi-coloured costume with a green wool cap entertains a gathering of little ones in a muddy field, leading them through a patch of undergrowth to inspect a charming fluffy white rabbit in closeup. The children watch the recorded presentation enrapt and join in the chorus of the familiar theme song.

Today The presenters laugh and joke amongst themselves, maintaining a relaxed and carefree atmosphere in the morning programme prior to introducing the first studio guest.

The presenters laugh and joke amongst themselves, maintaining a relaxed and carefree atmosphere in the morning programme prior to introducing the most recent summary of events.

The presenters laugh and joke amongst themselves, maintaining a relaxed and carefree atmosphere in the morning programme after the departure of the studio guest.

The presenters laugh and joke amongst themselves, maintaining a relaxed and carefree atmosphere in the morning programme.

Raincoat A round beige button slots neatly through the brass edged opening on the bulky canvas overcoat. A broad belt secures the waist, the material draped evenly over a dark blue suit. Mottled hands grip the knees for stability and the heavy jowled face registers discomfort as the man perspires profusely in the close heat of the compartment. To his side a self-possessed gentleman relaxes with a cigarette, head back, savouring the aroma, a lock of straight grey hair loose over the brow, a black raincoat folded on an attache case.

Walkers Her broad rear sways in soft camel slacks as she promenades with an escort along the avenue. Brilliant sunlight casts hard black shadows on the trees and highlights lemon foliage. The red bonnet of a sports car parked near the riverside gleams through the branches. Couples move slowly in the intense heat of late afternoon.

Licking A man settles himself on a low fence behind the superstore and removes the lid of a small ice cream tub. His long pink tongue flicks in and out, licking up the contents. A tub of rhubarb fool is consumed, the tongue licking remaining smears until mist on the metal surface clears and the spoon is restored to its silver gleam.
Incident and a Series An urgent report of a devastating incident is immediately followed by an update of the well-loved country series.

An urgent report of a devastating incident on the front page is compared with an update of a major golf tournament series on the back.

City In the darkness of early morning can be heard the continuous hum of traffic moving along the main routes into the city.

Eating The child in a high chair drops its bottle to the floor and a fizzing spray of Coke jets from the rubber teat over the maroon carpet. The family continues their meal undisturbed, forking large sections of pizza into their mouths and catching strands of melted cheese that adheres to their chins. They pause to draw on cigarettes left smouldering on saucers and divide the remnants of the main course. Outside a man walks by the window, his mouth stretched wide open as he attempts to swallow a whole pork pie.

Sausages Browning sausages sizzle and spit jets of boiling fat towards the orange bars of the grill. Skins blacken and crisp, baking in the intense heat of the oven.

Small Dreams In a forest clearing a band of explorers come upon a large black bomb set vertically on a plinth. They encircle the object and link arms in an attempt to carry it away. In the darkened subway a tube train arrives and crowds of passengers force an entry through buckled steel doors. In the corner of a compartment a traveller excitedly describes his recent experiences and achievements to a leading movie star who stands impassive by the window, elegant in a long cream coat.

Platform A panel of experts is seated in comfortable padded armchairs arranged in a semi-circle on a low platform surrounded by microphones. The camera scans each individual as they make considered contributions to the debate, when invited by the presenter, who occasionally refers to another party, their large face staring expectantly from a backdrop screen.

Train Passing The man ruffles his newspaper, folding it in a manner to obscure the contents from his neighbour's prying glance. On the other platform a girl adjusts the strap of her shoulder bag and turns to check the information on an overhead sign. Two workmen share a cigarette and a can of lager while silently watching the empty line.***'716359'***, the number depicted in yellow on blue flashes by, blurring into a continuous band on the side of a train passing through the station.

Fish Bar "It'll be ready in a few minutes." The customer waits at a spare table and studies the prices on a backlit sign. Deep yellow textured ceramic tiles decorate the walls, coordinated with red vinyl benches and cream floor tiles. An empty Coke can is deposited beside a serviette dispenser. The gaming machine bleeps repeated signals by the door. Winking lights flash in sequence: ***tokens-trail-pound-nudge-silver-jackpot..*** The invitation is ignored by the man at the counter who places his order and stands aside, hands thrust deep in his pockets, as he examines disinterestedly the encrusted objects spread for consumption in a heated glass cabinet.

Businessmen As darkness falls the businessmen leave their place of work and return to the underground car park. Yellow circular lights gleam on the rows of saloons. They approach their cars, first checking the tyres, then releasing the automatic locks with key codes. They remove their jackets and carefully hang them on side window hooks. Cases are deposited on adjacent seats and they relax at the wheel before securing safety belts and activating the lights and engines, to depart in order up the ramp towards the exit.

Greeting "What time of day do you call this then ?" An elderly man greets his comrade as they coincide on a street corner. They exchange a few words before a final salute and continue their various journeys, hobbling away slowly with the support of walking sticks.

Open Door Below the embankment leafy vines curl around an old brick wall. Branches hang heavy with foliage, shading the parapet and concealing the pointed arch of a small door. Fading green paint peels from its warped boards. It lies open, giving way to a dark recess wherein two large bins stand, filled with dead leaves and clipping from a long gardens.

Dogs Slavering dogs rush to a proffered bowl of compressed meat, lovingly attended by their keeper who explains the attraction and benefits of the particular product. A bedraggled sheep rears up from a slimy pit while, in the background, farmworkers can be seen approaching from a nest of cottages as the familiar theme tune introduces the well-loved country series. In a light comedy the young woman nervously rearranges the coffee table and checks her appearance in anticipation of her new escort's arrival. The camera tracks through offices and down corridors, closely following the detectives as they energetically pursue their routine. A man stretches and leans back in his swivel chair, satisfied with the solution to his problem which appears on the visual display.

Cable The traveller glances nervously as he shows up in a flash of headlights. Feet step over a yellow cable which snakes away into the darkness. Workmen shout and laugh at each other. One drags a heavy trolley of equipment, the other carries an empty pot of tar, stacking conical warning signs to the side as he clears the road for the waiting traffic. Steam rises from the freshly laid surface. Past a crushed '*Azda*' carton and floating strips of polythene wrapping. A long streak of mud trails from wheel tracks which recede on damp grey paving stones. Feet step over a yellow cable which snakes away into the darkness.

Dawn Silver frost glitters on the gravel surface, icy patches making a treacherous journey for the unwary. A heavy mist obscures the barrier of the weir, pale winter sun spreads pink ripples on a silent river. Beyond the great barge and a floating barrel stands a lone fisherman, his line stretched taut in the water. On the bridge a well wrapped girl steers her bicycle with care along the narrow gangway. Early morning walkers gather to converse as their dogs search the undergrowth. Wheels crackle the grass and pebbles on the sandy track over common land, turning onto the high road that runs by a small cluster of modest dwellings.

Dusk The evening sun sinks behind red clouds in the deepening sky, casting fiery gleams into the water. A tall figure looms, jogging by along the bank. Near the bridge, lines of twinkling lights show up raised hulks in the boatyards. Little people hurry across to the security of the riverside tavern while others continue on their homeward route.

Cork A cork explodes and flies away from an upturned bottle and sparkling liquid gushes from the slender neck into a clear crystal glass. Cascades of little bubbles surge towards the foaming surface in ceaseless waves. A langorous model drapes herself on a gilded chair, mysterious in black, her long legs crossed at the ankles, her face obscured by a purple silk veil. She arises and sweeps through palatial halls, pausing to strike a dramatic pose as a large flask of perfume comes into view. Cats curl before the flickering hearth and delicate fingers reach into an alluring tray of dark chocolates as hymns enhance the seasonal gift.

A cork explodes and flies away from an upturned bottle and sparkling liquid gushes from the slender neck into a clear crystal glass.
Shadows An upturned trolley lies in the gutter of the empty street. Trails of paper blow from a split bag of garbage. A group of men gathers by a red saloon, shadowy figures move in the darkness. A single street lamp illuminates the junction of two avenues.

Night Party Gusts of wind rattle the loose catch of the side gate and bang the garage door. The continuous beat of an all-night party is interspersed with shrieks and shouts of revellers on the estate. Puffs of pink clouds scurry across the darkened sky.

Part Seven

INTERVALS

1990

In the Park 1-2 The small terrier looks up from its investigation of an overflowing bin to watch three cheerful girls cycle past. A flock of pigeons gathers about an old woman, scrabbling for the crumbs she scatters in their path.

A heavily built man in black leather, bespectacled with a moustache, calls his dog and winds its leash in his hand, then boldly strides on, his wife hanging on his arm as she adjusts a warm grey scarf elegantly coiled about her head.

Diversion Bumpers of cars gleam in the nightlights. Yellow beams flash and criss-cross on the busy routes. On the right, traffic comes to a standstill and pedestrians quickly follow the signal to make for the other side. The bus proceeds through a darkened tunnel of temporary hoardings to cross the river at Blackfriars, giving a brief glimpse of imposing centres of commerce, reflected in green and orange ripples in the river. It turns again down unfamiliar side streets, past an illuminated maze of scaffolding and derelict shop fronts. "A temporary diversion, I'm afraid, the usual bridge is closed. We shall reach your destination." The driver reassures confused passengers. The grand entrance of Waterloo Station is sighted and a crowd of weary travellers is deposited, to find their way along windblown street and by narrow passages to gain access to the platforms.

Marketing "We are on-line to meet projected figures in the target areas." The young man hands his account to the woman with ash blond hair who turns slowly through the document as they lunch in a small trattoria. "*You will note the innovation of..*" he continues, flushing nervously, countering the absence of her response. She smiles slightly and spoons some cream from a coffee into her mouth, then lights another cigarette, dropping back her head to savour the aroma.

Cold Evening The newsvendor blows his hands against the cold evening as he guides a group of excited girls towards the main square. A band of merry buskers occupies a vacant arch behind the theatre, entertaining their audience with a medley of popular tunes. A boy and girl arrange themselves under thick blankets for the night, while continuing to beg for assistance from passers by. In a low-lit window of a chic restaurant a couple exchange fond glances and hold hands between dishes, deep in private conversation. A pair of plastic punk mannequins leer and beckon from their stand in the entrance to the show bar. A gang of drunken youths staggers over the road, jostling visitors who hurry away up darkened side streets from the centre.

In the Gutter After the heavy rain a stream of murky brown water swirls towards an open drain, carrying with it curls of paper, discarded wrapping, cigarette butts, a small crushed bright green can, dead and mouldering leaves, which have collected in the gutter of the high road, below the kerb of the pavement.

Soft-Fire A pretty child brings soft white tissues to comfort an aged relative who bends over domestic chores. A glamorous new car speeds along mountain highways and deep valleys. It travels by tumbling waterfalls, through charming peasant villages and golden wheat fields in the distant country. A large sign explodes into fire as it passes. The old woman wipes her eyes with the particular tissue and smiles fondly at the pretty child who waits expectantly in the sunlit doorway for her recovery.

Poor and Hungry A tall man in faded denim, pullover and track shoes, approaches the counter of the cafe. A young girl watches nervously from the door. His woman holds a whimpering baby to her shoulder for comfort while she indicates possible choices on the board. "How much would be two hamburgers? And how much an egg on toast? If we had a soup, a tea and a milk shake, what would that come to?" "£7.10p" the manager replies. The man leans on the counter pondering, then turns to consult with his family. After a whispered conversation they open the cafe door and depart up the high road. The proprietor shrugs and turns to serve the next customer. The hand toys with a fresh scoop of spaghetti coiled around the fork, and adds more grated cheese to complement the flavour of a rich meat sauce.

Working A fair haired girl nestles a telephone between her neck and shoulder and smiles prettily during the confidential call. On an upper level, a striking woman in a fitted black skirt and bright yellow patterned blouse checks a document, then moves towards the door. In an adjacent window a man in shirtsleeves consults with his colleagues on a particular matter of business, while, in reception, the commissionaire waits respectfully by the entrance as senior executives bid farewell to a party of visiting clients.

Gathering Two women are seated on a large sofa. They converse gaily, admiring each other's presentation, occasionally touching hands and hair. A man enters the room, smartly dressed in a light suit. They acknowledge his arrival with warm smiles and survey him with interest. A younger woman in a blue and white print skirt appears at a side door and moves towards the gathering. They all greet her. The man gives a look of intimate recognition and embraces her. The women on the sofa exchange significant glances and signal the moment to leave the couple to their own devices.

An excited group of friends and relatives await the limousine which carries the bride to her wedding ceremony. Guests crowd around the happy girl and garland her with flowers. An elderly man relaxes contented in an armchair as the scene closes. Titles signal the end of the soap, relayed in silence from twelve TVs stacked in the window of the hire centre.

Question Bands of images and titles flash past, intercut with brief extracts from the forthcoming schedule of entertainment. In a sports quiz a young man in a brightly patterned pullover stares ahead, morose and silent, mouth open, unable to frame an answer to the question.

In Silence "But surely it's obvious that the government deprives.." One of the women at a lunch party eagerly addresses a colleague, then smiles and tosses her hair, excited by his confusion. The other girl languidly explores her tall glass of ice cream, delving to the bottom with a long spoon to retrieve some raspberry sauce. The senior man in the group maintains a cool distance from the debate, faintly amused by the animated discussion. He lights another cigarette and regards the girl in silence as she closes her eyes, savouring the dessert.

Passing A small white statuette stands on a pedestal in the garden of the terrace cottage. Tangled branches and leaves are gathered in a barrow near the back fence, ready for burning. Between the buildings can be seen a bright parade of shops. Busy traffic comes to a halt at the junction of the high street to allow for a change of flow. High red brick walls of the business centre give way to a dilapidated tenement, broad green stains running down the crumbling balconies, broken windows revealing the black space of empty rooms. ***"Trolley Park"***, a bold brown and yellow sign indicates the rack for customer's containers in the back lot of the superstore. Sunlight catches the ribbed roof of a long storage hangar. A plane climbs steadily in the clear sky above blue blocks of a high rise development. ***"Taro-Stax-Enero"***, intricate signatures in striking black and white designs embellish a low concrete wall that borders the track linking suburban stations.

Cashpoint "Didn't you know, she's gone on a world tour promotion." The girl in black leotards and leather jacket converses with her friend as she operates the cashpoint, "this week France, Italy and Spain. Next week, New York and L.A., all over the place." "That's great," enthuses her companion who then falls silent, her red lacquered lips pursed with envy at the thought of the success. "Oh drat it!" The card is returned by the machine, refusing credit. "It's okay, we'll get some money over here." The girl searches her bag for a chequebook and joins the queue for counter service.

Arts and Entertainment Brightly coloured titles and images flash and interchange. The smooth features of the popular presenter appear. The young man in a pale pink jacket and pencil tie lounges in a soft padded swivel chair, picking his nose for amusement and exchanging casual banter with his technical assistants. He introduces a preview of his new series. Two men in conventional attire face each other in a darkened space, raising their legs in slow motion to perform ritual movements. In a bright white studio youths and girls hop and jig about, driven to high excitement by a relentless staccato beat. Cartoon characters and layers of textured patterns intersperse the several extracts, raising interest in the lively mixture of arts and entertainment.

Eating A fair-haired girl in a polka dot skirt and black tights listens to her companion's confidences wide-eyed while spooning large portions of yoghurt from a plastic tub, her reflection divided in the dark window of the compartment.

Watching A man taps the point of his neatly rolled umbrella on the carriage floor and impatiently shuffles the contents of his case, watching for a sign of movement in the train, on his homeward journey.

Sleeping Her head slips downward, tousled brown hair spread over an open collar. Fingers toy unconsciously with a wooden toggle at the end of a long cord. She slumps sideways, leaning against the glass partition, the bright yellow, red, green and violet sections of her jacket reflected in several layers in the dark window of the compartment.

In Service A waiter hovers attentively, adjusting the tableware and proffering a bottle of wine for approval. Another moves forward and sprinkles a little pepper to enhance a starter of finely sliced avocado and mozzarella, then retires to a respectful distance as the men continue to discuss matters of importance, while appreciating the various courses of their meal.

Display A fine display of cameras, video machines and sundry accessories tempts the passer-by into a specialist shop where he views gleaming racks of varied products and special discount offers. The assistant raises himself from the floor where he kneels, attempting to connect wires to a socket. He appears tired and unshaven, his tie askew with white shirt loose around a sagging middle. He stands open-mouthed, appearing not to comprehend the potential customer's enquiry.

Standing Man Broad shoulders of a dark green flecked suit drop slightly to the left. Smartly cut ginger hair is brushed back, clipped close to the neck above the collar of a fresh blue striped cotton shirt. The main weight rests on the right hip with the left leg casually extended. One hand holds a rolled newspaper, the other, an early morning cigarette. Well pressed trousers fold on polished brogues completing an impression of quiet assurance in the standing man, as he waits on the platform of the suburban station to commence the schedule of the day's assignments.

Simple A gangling youth relaxes, stretching long legs onto the opposite seat, nudging the girl in the corner and amusing her with casual banter. She regards him with interest, allowing his approaches. He delves in his bag and suddenly produces a detached bicycle seat which he waves in the air, causing her to drop her ice cream down her front and to collapse in loud laughter.

Fairground Tough girls with ringlet hair, black jeans and leather jackets, hustle for custom at their stalls.."*Dare the Black Box..Ghost House..Try your luck sir, a prize for everyone.*" Plastic hoops too small to encircle the objects, darts too light to reach their target.."*Ring a duck and win a soft toy.*" The Great Girator loops ever larger spirals with its attached compartments spinning in counter motion. Squeals of excitement rise from the Wall of Death as its occupants are flattened to the sides by increasing speed. Small children grip the safety bars of giant teacups that rotate and roll up and down on the mechanical roundabout.

New Car He turns to the pretty woman beside him and smiles, then concentrates on the journey. She returns his affectionate glance and leans back, relaxing in a comfortable seat. She angles her head to check the children who respond with gay laughter. The camera withdraws to a great distance to record the image of the elegant new car that speeds along a broad highway, through a deserted landscape and into the sunset.

Walkway A sudden shower sweeps over the walkway that runs by the railway line on Waterloo Bridge. Pedestrians hold their coats close and grasp umbrellas suddenly reversed in the cross-winds. A group of tourists looks down between heavy girders at the murky green water and patches of debris carried along in the swirling current. "*Spare a penny sir?*" Two young men waiting by the exit accost an office worker hurrying home, and restrain their large alsatian, leashing it to the railings.

Sunday A girl in dark glasses relaxes at a cafe table in the brilliant sunshine, resting her feet on an adjacent chair as she leafs through a selection of papers. Casual sightseers pause to inspect a collection of bric-a-brac in the darkened window of a second-hand shop and gay fabrics displayed in a small boutique. A man strides past, clenching and unclenching his fist as he returns from his morning exercise.

Quid pro Quo "So we shift him out of insurance and over to department, then infill our man as the new operative." Two men plan their strategy for imminent changes at work. The senior associate listens to the proposal, tapping his pen in time with the beat of a neighbour's tape."*Hello everybody !"* Teenage girls crowd through a connecting door and spread themselves on spare seats, blowing large pink bubbles from their gum as they eye the available talent. "..and quid pro quo, we move in and clear the fucking lot." The younger man laughs and lounges back in his seat while his colleage remains silent, biting his knuckle as he ponders the implications of the solution.

In Sunlight A man in faded jeans and a checked shirt engages a woman in conversation, leaning casually against his red saloon. Sunlight plays on his silver hair and reflects in his tinted glasses, in a car park by riverside gardens near Shepperton.

Well built, of mature years, wearing a green aertex shirt and cream slacks, he assumes the correct position for his drive from the tee. His woman waits at a short distance, observing the performance with interest and admiring the confident stance of his figure in the sunlight.

Bond Street Fattish legs are cased in brown silk stockings. A short beige cape is swept to the left, secured with a jewelled clasp over a matching skirt. She holds her head high, her long ash blond hair casually tied with a black lace ribbon. Tinted glasses shield watchful eyes and an even tanned complexion. She strides purposefully down Bond Street, ignoring the varied window displays: in one , a charming full length Edwardian bridal gown with pearl button shoes; in another, the latest fashions from leading designers; a showcase of master paintings and antique furniture; racks of perfume and jewellery; gentlemen's accessories, and the occasional blacked-out interior, sadly indicating a business recently departed.

The Boat The detective looks pleased as they pull alongside the large white boat, moored in the blue waters of the bay. His face turns down, tucking into the collar of a crumpled raincoat. The shadowed fold of his rugged jaw creases towards hooded eyes, wrinkled with an amused and quizzical expression.

Lights flash and criss-cross the surface of the black waters as divers search for evidence to assist the case. The detective sits on a bollard on the quayside and lights the fresh cigar clamped in his mouth, hunching with concentration as he ponders a solution.

A drunken woman slumps forward over the bar table. She weeps and runs her hand through her hair, harassed by persistent questions, while the detective watches in silence from the corner of the room.

Shoppers "My dear, do you mind my dogs? So kind of you.." A tall woman in white smiles at the patient girl by the counter and leads her pair of pet spaniels around the store while her husband picks through a pile of slacks on offer in the discount sale. Young mothers with children struggle up the winding stairs, weighed down with packages. A mature man in a navy blazer, pink shirt and pale grey cords, drifts among the racks of designer wares, absorbing the lively rhythm of caribbean disco, relayed through several speakers.

Portobello A girl in dark glasses and a bright yellow scarf rests her arm on the door of an open top sports car and leans back, enjoying the mid-afternoon heat as she waits at the top of the Portobello Road. Groups of kids in gaily patterned T-shirts and shorts with backpacks and head-phones, wander from shop to shop,crowding into small boutiques and reverberating record stores. Lines of vivid posters project unknown entertainers from dilapidated walls and boarded windows of disused premises. Visitors turn through stalls of bric-a-brac and take their ease in sidewalk cafes while local residents linger on street corners, passing discreet and amiable conversation.

Young Ones Her pretty oval face is framed with a mass of dark curls. She leans on his arm and gazes up affectionately as he embraces her. Her lilac flowered top and orange shorts contrast with his black and yellow striped sweatshirt and white jeans. Lean and agile, carrying a folded newspaper under his arm, he leads her as they casually stroll up the high street, laughing at their little dog bounding along beside.

Sunlight and Shadows Broad shadows are cast from an avenue of chestnut trees with patches of brilliant sunlight that illuminate the figures of two bold lads who stride ahead, engaged in animated conversation, past groups of office workers enjoying their lunch hour at boulevard cafes along the high road.

Riverside Tangled branches of a fallen tree submerge in the mildewed surface of a still dark pool in a shady grove below the narrow track. Stone walls of the causeway descend in stepped levels to shale borders of the winding river. On the far side gleam lines of cars parked about the old church tower of Isleworth. A man in a dark suit walks slowly along, taking in the pleasant views on his way. On the Regency style terraces of Richmond, couples promenade and gather in lively conversation before the popular wine bar. Young women in bright summer dresses vie for the attention of their escorts, while mothers with children and elders rest on grassy banks under spreading chestnuts and poplars, watching the progress of boat crowded with trippers that pass on the glittering waters.

Meat Counter "A little bit over, but will that do?" The dapper master butcher weighs a string of sausages and bundles them up for the customer. The queue passes amiable observations of local events while the women carefully inspect the bloodied joints of meat on display behind the glass counter. "Looks nice, doesn't it?" A girl remarks at the bus stop outside as several waves of fighter planes fly past in immaculate formation

Judging The younger man adopts a deferential manner as he introduces the eminent guests. Three chefs attend to their dishes, hurriedly preparing an inventive menu for the experts' assessment. The team approaches the table and prods with spoons and forks to detach a portion of the presented dish. The cooks wait at the side, watching for signs of appreciation, twitching nervously at remarks passed on the effect and quality of each part - comments mumbled through filled cheeks. One judge slices at a rack of lamb with a long knife, tearing meat from the bone with his teeth as he returns to a padded armchair on a platform in the studio.

Big Cake A wreath of golden chopped nuts rests on a generous layer of whipped cream, moulded into little waves laced with fragments of chocolate wafer. The porous texture of the light sponge sparkles with a hint of strawberry. Towards the centre lies a rich confection of fruit, concealed within the enticing creation. Beyond the big slab of cake a young woman reclines on a sunbed, lost in a pleasant mood of dreamy contentment under a bright blue sky.

Red Van A sheen of fine drizzle casts up gleams on the black tarmac, cross-cut with reflections of passing traffic. Late shoppers shuffle back and forth in the darkness, steering loaded trolleys. A street lamp illuminates the bulky presence of a red van parked by the entrance to the superstore, amplifying a long scrape and dent in its side.
The Traveller "Which way to Hammersmith, mate?" A man in white shirt-sleeves leans to the open window of his saloon to address a passer-by. Finding his route he returns to the wheel and departs with screeching tyres, turning in a broad arc back towards the city.

1991

Cream and Grey Sundry reading matter, a street guide, light novels, a scatter of correspondence, lies disordered on the bedside cabinet. A row of switches avails the visitor of a varied choice of entertainment. The net veil shifts slightly in the soft breeze through a half-open window that reveals a pleasant aspect of leafy shrubbery, with a fountain playing in the small gardens.

A half-finished glass of orange with a flexible blue striped straw stands beside the cream telephone, beyond a grey metal container of water, on the side table.

Magenta and Yellow At the appointed hour a smartly presented girl appears to relay information of the day. Her lightly curled hair accords prettily with a brilliant magenta cardigan, that vibrates against a chrome yellow background.

White and Red Lithe female athletes in gaily patterned slips take their places at the starting blocks. They bend forward and flex their calves, spare frames tensed, awaiting orders. Gleaming white lines on a rust red ground mark the several lanes of the stadium.

Red and Brown The pretty girl in a red T shirt tosses her mane of glossy dark brown hair and smiles softly as she selects the appropriate brand of conditioner from a row of empty plastic bottles.

White and Blue A fluffy white kitten snuggles under the warm duvet between a sleeping couple in a double bed. In the kitchen it waits eagerly as its owner deposits the contents of a can of its favourite food into a blue bowl on the floor. It lies back as a comb is gently drawn through a delicate coat of white fur, to demonstrate its fine condition.

Red and Gold A giant spoon delves into a richly textured mound to retrieve a perfectly shaped scoop of chocolate ice, then coated with a glutinous, toffee-like substance, poured from above. In a moment of transformation it becomes an impressive oblong bar, wrapped with the familar red and gold insignia of the well-known confection.

Black and White **£10.99**. The bold graphic statement declares a bargain price for ceramic wall tiles, advertised in the morning paper. On an adjacent page a young woman's happy smile signifies her joy at the hero's return. Two fine vertical lines break the mechanical dot screen which scans the evenly spaced teeth of the girl's happy smile.

White and Black **6, 7, 15, 16**. District forecasts predict the day's conditions and summarize weather patterns. Below, a small white crescent set within a sharp black square depicts the moon rising.

Soft Orange The woman turns to regard an admirer who addresses her gently from the door. He enquires her thoughts and plans, and moves towards her for closer contact. She hesitates and avoids his approach, picking up instead a white cup of coffee, sensing the aroma with languid appreciation. She then raises her face towards his, they almost touch in the soft orange fireside glow.

Lilac and Green A lilac band overlays the emerald green pitch, giving continuous updates of the state of play. Men in visored helmets and padded armour confront each other in a contest of precise skills. The crowd urges on the competitors with long grunts and howls of support and disappointment. Repeated recordings allow exacting study of key points of play, which expert commentators clarify with additional information. The image of a batsman is suspended, allowing three sequential views of the bowler's fast delivery. Action replays from several angles allow detailed analysis of the key incident, which experts clarify with additional information.

Lilac and Green A lilac band overlays the emerald pitch, giving continuous updates of the state of play.

Green and White Brilliant flashes of tracer fire flare up in the night sky, white streaks disrupting a grainy green ground.

Yellow and Blue A couple settle on the beach and arrange their picnic. The woman discourages the young man's eager advances, brushing away strands of tawny hair from her finely set cheekbones, and looking coolly into the distance. Later they stroll arm in arm, engaged in deep discussion to resolve their problems. Evening light catches a dip in the deep yellow sand, set against the steady wash of an azure blue ocean.

Blue and Grey An elderly man and woman face each other across the kitchen table. She addresses a searching question, which he finds hard to answer. His face looms larger, perspiring, mouth hanging open, eyes vacant, his blue tie askew between the lapels of a pale grey jacket.

Grey and Orange In the early dawn heavy drapes are silhouetted before a part-open window. Vertical bands of grey light filter the translucent net veil, picking up reflected orange tints from a single spotlight in the small gardens.

Pink and Cream The rattle of a tea trolley signals the commencement of the day, as attendants engage in lively chatter in the corridors.The young woman busies herself arranging a bouquet of fresh flowers in the room. A cup angles slightly towards an empty dish and spoon, sides flecked with the remains of cereal. A glass of fruit juice stands untouched by the coffee pot. Beyond the milk jug a pretty array of little sugar packets, ranging from white to orange and pink, stacked in a small bowl set on a cream paper base.

Part Eight

CROSS CONNECTIONS

1995

Woman in Black The woman in black sharply presses her neighbour's elbow off the arm rest that divides their seats in the corner of the compartment. She breathes heavily, sharp snorts of exhaled air registering a certain aggravation at the proximity of the man. Her broad fleshy shoulders are tightly contained within a smartly fitted black jacket. Of substantial build, tall and imposing, her thighs are pressed firmly together in a short fitted skirt and stockings. She maintains precedence in the seats, spreading her arms sideways to gain maximum space, as she dramatically flips pages of a magazine and newspaper. An unconfined impatience permeates her haughty demeanor, particularly apparent when her subsidiary neighbour inadvertently coughs and burps, catching his breath.

Stations pass and she maintains her place, unyielding and highly tensed. *Emotional Features,* brightly decked women pose prettily in the glossy layouts of the popular magazine. It merely seems to further irritate the woman in black, whose manicured fingers trail over the surface, snatching the corner of the page to flick on through the magazine, then, as suddenly, switching to her newspaper, flapping its loose large pages in her neighbour's face. She appears to be profoundly aware of the man's presence, even though he restricts himself politely to the smallest possible space. Her instability and impatience become apparent to other passengers, who note her behaviour with significant glances.

The man retreats as far as possible into the corner, pressing himself against the partition of the carriage, but still the woman reminds him of her presence, tensing at his every movement. Her long legs, cased in dark stockings and shiny well-heeled shoes, are kept securely together, exuding an intense pressure and warmth, almost in frustrated invitation.

She both demands and resists attention, arching her back and pressing for maximum space and gravity, yet constantly failing to gain satisfaction from her physical situation. This causes her even greater agitation, expressed in the rapid creasing of her reading matter and ever more insistent breathing. The man remains paralysed, motionless, avoiding any action with extreme care. Aware of the potentially dangerous situation he fixes his gaze on a neutral aspect of the compartment, away from his dominant neighbour. The end-stop approaches and the compartment prepares to exit. The woman in black makes great play of tidying her papers, snap-catching her brown leather briefcase and sorting its contents. She remains seated as long as possible, guarding her territorial space, and finally, as the carriage clears, she raises herself to her full height, fearsome and magnificent, and strides victorious from the battleground of the train to merge with the confused rush of the platform, flourishing her pass as she exits through the barrier.

Grab Large cranes, blue grey in the smoky atmosphere, dip and rise in a balletic ritual, grasping mounds of scrap metal and depositing them on top of the heap. The flattened carcasses of whole crushed cars float skyward and crash into place on a mountain of machine parts. Long rusted pipes spread in stacked mounds along the banks above the tracks. Trains rush to and fro on their journeys, below the bridge at Willesden Junction.

Man and Boy The man leaves a small terrace house and moves from the flowered trellis gate towards his car. Tall, well-built, in his mid-thirties, in smart sports wear: aertex shirt, shorts, trainers. He steps in a slightly diagonal direction, hand reaching in his pockets for keys, preparing to unlock the car. A young boy appears beyond the man. He is about nine years old, in a lilac T shirt and black nylon slacks. He progresses along the pavement in a curious irregular motion; walking, stopping, breaking into a short run, twisting, turning, dipping on and off the kerb. The distance closes to about five yards from the man, who turns back from his car with a sheaf of Sunday papers under his arm, shutting the door with decision.The man returns to his house, entering the porch. The boy's image crosses his imposing figure; lighter, amused and preoccupied, following his own dreamed footsteps. They pass each other, the man entering his house, the boy continuing to meander along the road, switching his movements as in some private dance.

Crack of Light 1-2 Deep shadows obscure the brown blocked bars of wood that form the irregular framework of the battered door. A decorative tiled floor spans away in the darkness, its pattern reflected in the crack of light that gleams brilliantly in the gap between the closet door and the floor. Smooth and dark, the immaculate surface of a melamine faced partition spreads upwards into darkness. A useful hook for spare garments is faintly discerned projecting from the wall, caught in the crack of light that gleams brilliantly under the door of the closet.

Man and Door A salesman in a dark blue suit stands on the shortpathway to the terraced house. He faces a dark green door, closed with drawn net curtains on the small paned windows. His stance is firm and motionless, suspended in the hope that his call may still be answered.

Shelter She stands for shelter under the striped awning of a shop window, as rain sheets down in a passing shower. Her long black hair straggles damp over a brown cardigan. She occasionally draws on a cigarette and glances bleakly at the reflections cast by passing traffic in the high road. Long dark hair, spreads damp over a loose brown cardigan. Pale face under the striped awning of a shop window as she shelters from the rain that sheets down in a passing shower. She occasionally draws on a cigarette and glances bleakly at the reflections cast by passing traffic in the high road.

1996

Man in Grey "So what precisely is your function?" The man in a grey raincoat somewhat aggressively addresses his fellow traveller, a bespectacled woman who flushes defensively at his direct approach. "I am the product manager for the central area with additional responsibility for international relations." His demeanor remains cold and impassive, eyes fixed unblinking on her face. He stands rigidly by the carriage door, feet protecting a battered briefcase. "My weekends are now occupied with visits to my wife. She has been ill in hospital." His features register a momentary drop into an introspective mood, and are vested with an unfathomable weariness, as he turns to look vacantly at the passing landscape of the journey. The woman senses the change and softens her guard, gently probing the matter with a sympathetic enquiry, but he quickly steers the conversation back to professional matters, the basis of their initial engagement.

Blue Wall Minute crevises pit the dimly lit surface, with occasional chips fallen away to reveal the porous texture of the brickwork. The efficiently constructed partition is covered with a clear blue sheen of emulsion that offsets the firm upright block of varnished wood and strong brass hinges that frame the door to the private cubicle of the gentleman's closet.

Hotel, Jersey *23.12-28.12.97*

Poolside A man pedals vigorously on an exercise bicycle while children splash happily in the pool. Pleasant music of a seasonal nature emits from surrounding speakers. A vine of broad leaves clusters a column of the balustrade which surrounds the pool. Beach robes are flung casually over blue striped deck chairs. Children splash happily in the water while stormy gales spread the beach beyond. The man grips bars of a weight training machine and pulls them vigorously to his chest. Pleasant music of a seasonal nature emits from surrounding speakers. An elderly woman wears a light polythene cap to protect her hair as she swims back and forth, enjoying the heated water of the pool.

Headland Through the Parish Church Yard of St.Brelade's, where mouldering gravestones bear incised tributes to loved ones and mark their time of passing. The path leads around the headland, pink slab walls supporting mossy banks of gorse and heather. Holiday villas, cream-faced, enhanced with decorative ironwork, lie quiet in the winter season. A young girl passes on her horse, taking it down the slipway to ride on the sands. As the road curves upward a muddy side track drops away to a promentary with benches, giving a special viewpoint of the broad span of the bay. A fresh incoming breeze creates pearl breakers in the cool blue wash, where small dots of surfers brave a vigorous swell. The route terminates abruptly at the gated entrance to a private villa; a bold cut into the rocks makes a useful parking space, the rust red tarmac laid to a smooth finish.

At the Bar The assistant continues to wipe glasses and line them up in order on the bar, while chatting casually to a guest who leans on the counter.

The Maids The girls draw back the coverlet of the double bed to confirm its correct presentation.

Ice-Fish A magnificent leaping salmon made in solid ice decked with green lights rears above the buffet of assorted fruit, biscuits and nuts.

Headland 2 A fresh squall gusts in, scattering spray in rivulets over the beach and whipping up spats of sand in the walker's path. The headland looms against the patchy sky, rising up from a base of blackened shale and grit. Fractured blocks of the rockface are interspersed with rust red and green gorse and heather. A bungalow tucked into the peak tenaciously holds against the storm. The small settlement of cottages and holiday cafes below sits quiet in the wintry season. A red earth rock stands separate from the bulk of the headland, set on an outcrop of shale and grit battered by the rising swell.

Shaft of Sunlight A shaft of sunlight spreads a triangle of bright green over the cool grey ocean. A shaft of sunlight spreads a span of bright green over the warm grey ocean.

A shaft of sunlight spreads bands of pale cream, breaking the warm blue shade of the windswept sands.Specks of white light scatter in the walker's path as shafts of sunlight break the warm blue shade of the windswept sands.

The walker returns a signal of greeting from a companion on the hotel balcony, crossing the windswept sands in an early morning outing.

The Family The family forms a neat rectangle, seated in order around a long table. The father, a grey-whiskered nautical type of genial energy, leans towards his elegant wife, attractive in a soft woollen twin set. To their right quietly sits their younger daughter. The elder son, a bold young man of fine bearing, wears a dark dress suit with immaculate white cummerbund and bow tie. He converses gently with his grandmother, while the other daughter remains detached, sitting straight backed in her chair, eyes lowered to her plate, as she carefully sections a piece of meat for consumption.

Board Game "Whatever you may want to do you are obliged to take me." The man instructs his partner in the board game. 'Otherwise you will just be huffing.' Interjects their companion who follows the game from the side.

Coffee Order 'Are you hand-grinding those beans?' The lady enquires after her coffee order. 'It will soon be time to syringe my ears again.' Her companion renews their topic of conversation.

Family 2 The fair-haired child coughs repeatedly while his father continues to work his way methodically through the midday meal. The child wanders from the table and his grandmother follows to steer him back to his seat. The pretty mother engages in friendly conversation with a neighbour while her husband looks ahead, continuing to methodically clear his plate.

Buffet Kitchen assistants in blue caps and aprons clear uneaten food from the poolside buffet, transferring large wedges of lemon cheesecake to the trolley for disposal. "I want to go up not down." A sweating house manager instructs his staff as they struggle to shift heavy boxes of wine bottles onto a small ramp leading to another section.

Cabaret With a slight of hand Toni the Magician removes a chair from beneath the substantial figure of the prone blonde assistant, leaving her apparently suspended in thin air, to appreciative applause of the evening dinner guests. With a slight of hand Toni the Magician spins rings and fans of cards, and produces a clutch of doves from his tailcoat, to appreciative applause from the evening dinner guests. The pretty girl with bobbed auburn hair extends her tongue to share a spoon of sugared dessert with her companion, licking her lips in appreciation.

The pretty girl with bobbed hair toys dreamily with a giant extended lime green balloon, fondly nestling her cheek against the smooth inflated surface.

Headland 3 Early morning light breaks over the headland casting long reflections on the damp sands.

Waiting The woman in a brown striped cardigan and slacks sits quietly in a cane chair, looking amiably towards reception as she waits for the next event in the day.

A man in a blue shirt and pullover sits quietly in a cane chair, looking amiably towards the restaurant as he waits for the next event in the day. The woman in brown and the man in blue face each other and engage in quiet conversation, as the waiter carefully places a tea tray on the round glass topped table.

Evening Blocks of brown and grey shadows appear suspended in the enfolding gloom of a rainy evening in a suburban side road. Continuous drizzle casts up bright uneven reflections on the pavement and in the gutter.

Strings of twinkling lights illuminate random objects with striking effect a pair of intricate pale blue wrought iron gates; the white bonnet of a parked transit van; black and silver garbage bags stacked neatly for collection. The small black dog snuffles in the grass verge and jumps back, agitated by the impact of two young girls who whip by on rollerblades, chattering and laughing, followed at a distance by their mother, short and breathless, in the soft pillow of a dark blue anorak.

On the Bus A young man lounges comfortably across the seats, feet propped on a bar as he studies the day's sport's fixtures. Wizened features of a senior citizen are reflected in the glass partition, her polyester rain hat tied over a firm grey perm. The blackness of a man's jacket resonates against the maroon upholstery of the interior. The bus halts and passengers disembark; as the doors close a young woman panics, unable to negotiate the exit with her children, shopping and a folded buggy. The bus moves off to expressions of concern from fellow travellers. Annoyed, the man in black remonstrates with the driver.

Room "It's alright my dear, I'll get them." Solicitous of his wife's condition in the later days of the illness the man volunteers to collect the particular volumes from the bookshelf in the front room. The door opens to the aspect of a broad white space, large plate windows covered with a net veil of muslin drapes giving onto a quiet suburban side road. Caught by the peaceful atmosphere the man pauses and moves to a single desk by the window, slipping into an introspective mood of a half dream. Sitting at the desk he toys absent-minded with some ornament, his mind passing on no particular course of action.

Gradually he gives himself up to silent waves of varied pressure emanating from the surrounding space. To his right the curved alcove which frames a period pine chest a soft cream band of sunlight warms the walls, dropping in the corner to a blue shade. The sensations of the room are not however entirely comfortable. With prickling anticipation the man becomes aware of conflicting elements, the natural warmth of the late summer afternoon intercepted by a bar of cold air that settles like an uninvited guest and shifts imperceptibly across the interior. A deadening weight of increased pressure lays on the frontal lobes of his forehead, spreading a sheen of nervous sweat over his skin surface.

Trying to shake off this elusive presence he turns his attention to the view beyond, to a small tree planted in the forecourt . The man concentrates his whole energy on the tree, staring hard at the junction of the trunk and first branches with their sparse beginning of curled leaves. Held rigid to the desk, fingers gripping its edge, and subject to rising ripples of dynamic impulses he is no longer able to conrol his responses. Involuntary surges pass from the pivot of his breast bone and follow a magnetic path through the window to the small tree, transferring his pressure to another organism. Presently the emotion subsides and a quiet balance returns to his centre. He rises from the desk , retrieves the books from the shelf and retires from the room, leaving withered shrubs and a dying leafless tree in the modest planting area of the forecourt.

Silhouette Three figures recede in the darkness, silhouetted by lamplight through the archway on the towpath. A train roars by over the bridge while above passes the ghost of a nightflight. Three figures recede in the darkness, silhouetted by lamplight through the archway on the tow path. *Car-Cafe* Illuminated by the light of the Cafe a passing car with passengers moves slowly on to the junction.

Frill Two gulls swoop over a sparkling stretch of bright blue ocean; fresh white breakers frill the span of smooth blond beaches dotted with palm trees. The Statue of Liberty rises above New York Harbour emblazoned with a bold graphic sign of a budget travel break in a far country. A giant slice of tomato creamed with mayonnaise is gently lowered to join the spectacular silver band of an onion ring and deep green foliage of a lettuce leaf which rest on the vast planar surface of a sizzling beefburger. Globular drops of rich red sauce are squeezed from between the compressed massive round blocks of a soft yellow seeded bun.

A cheerful waitress clears the diners' plates and notes their choice of desserts. Illuminated by the light of the Cafe a passing car with passengers moves slowly to the junction.

High Road A young woman walks by along the windswept street, busy morning traffic passing in the high road. Brown shawl over cream skirt, long dark hair ruffled in the fresh breeze as she glances at the new fabric shop. Man moves across her path, preoccupied with his schedule of engagements, conversing with a colleague on his mobile phone. At the junction a red car moves forward. Roadsweeper leans on his broom staring reflectively into space and coughs, scratching the side of his nose.

The roadsweeper leans on his broom, scratches the side of his nose and coughs, staring reflectively into space. A fresh breeze ruffles the long dark hair of the young woman as she walks along the high road, pausing to glance at the new fabric shop.

A fresh breeze ruffles the long dark hair of the young woman as she pauses to glance at swatches of brightly printed material, on view in the new fabric shop in the high road.

Contacts "And I wish you good day sir." The Irishman replaces his receiver to cut the failed cold call to a potential client. The Irishman replaces the receiver to cut the failed cold call and engages in some casual banter with his colleagues before resuming his contact list.

In the Lift "One hour from Hounslow." The aggrieved woman relates the episode of her journey to work to a fellow traveller in the lift and sighs heavily. "I travel by bike." The listener responds, but the woman ignores the remark, caught up in the web of her own experience and she exits at the second level with a dour and determined expression.

Spring Showers "It's still there and I'm getting really hacked off about it." The fair-haired architect from the third floor leans on the counter in reception to report the continued leak from the glass roof into his office. Waves of sleet batter the temporary roof causing occupants to detach themselves from their monitors and gather interested around possible areas of damage.

"She will trample those with her pretty little foot." He observes the careful layout of documents on the floor, cautioning the bent back of a colleague to the entrance of the property manager.

Fresh Breeze A fresh breeze ruffles the long dark hair of the young woman who walks along the high road. A man exits from the glass door of an electrical hire shop and passes behind her, preoccupied in a private conversation with an unknown colleague on his mobile phone.

Her long dark hair is ruffled by a fresh breeze as she turns to glance at brightly printed materials on view in the fabric shop. She turns slightly on an impulse, caught by the view of brightly printed materials gathered in multi-coloured layers in the new fabric shop. Her long black hair is ruffled by a fresh breeze that gusts the high road. A man exits in her path from the glass door of an electrical hire shop, continuing a complex negotiation with an unknown colleague on his mobile phone.

His heavy jowled face and thickset build contained within a light grey suit. Hand grips a mobile phone close to continue a private conversation. Shoulders hunched as the head turns down to concentrate on details of the complex negotiation with an unknown colleague. He moves quickly from the glass door of an electrical hire shop in the high road, passing behind the young woman who glances at arrangements of pretty printed materials on view in the new fabric shop in the high road. The roadsweeper pauses in his work and leans on his broom. He stares reflectively into space and coughs, waiting for the next incident.

2000

Vampire Lovers embrace in a darkened room entwined in a loose sheet. The camera recedes, reducing the scene to a small cube. Panic spreads amongst the throng of partygoers as unseen forces cause vibrations through the house. A vine of sharpened leaves forces itself through cracks in the floorboards and cornices, and rapidly winds itself around the interior.

Radio Two women discuss a topic of mutual interest in lively and concerned tones. One dominates with a constant flow of information, the interviewer intercedes at intervals to probe particular details and steer the course of the conversation.

Edifice Tiny specks of visitors circulate in the cavernous arena of the new cultural edifice, and rise on silver escalators to the upper floors. In the passageways and galleries helpful attendants provide information about sundry exhibits. A man positions a camera on a heavy tripod to film little hammers that strike a mirrored wall in a particular sequence, while his colleague points a fur muffled microphone in the direction of an interested spectator.

View A corner of the spectator's overcoat appears in shimmering hues of orange and lemon, reflected in the glass of a vast paper pattern, presented in the new cultural edifice.

The dome of St.Paul's Cathedral and its surrounding buildings shimmer in bright sunlight across the river, viewed through tall windows of the new cultural edifice.

Sandwich A stack of cling-wrapped sandwiches offers varied fillings: egg mayonnaise, bacon and avocado, cheese and lettuce, all tempting the eye in the small buffet of an underground station.

Scent A girl stands listless in the empty perfume shop, surrounded by pretty jars and bottles.

Knockers "I wish to encourage charitable work between neighbours." A young woman with fair hair in a smart brown suit introduces herself on the doorstep. "I have no interest in charity", replies the occupier. Her pretty smile fades in surprise. She stands perplexed as he slowly closes the door on her.

"I'm John The Fish and I would like to explain what I have to offer." A fattish well-spoken man presents himself buoyantly in the early evening. "I have no interest in fish", the occupier replies as he places a half eaten plate of cod and chips on a side table by the door. The man steps back in shock, completely deflated by the response. "The best of luck with your venture", the occupier offers some encouragement before slowly closing the door.

A young man appears and waves a photo-card for identification. He mumbles an unintelligible message of his services. "I don't need anything", the occupier replies and slowly closes the door. The youth remains on the doorstep swaying from foot to foot, his features confused with blank incomprehension.

Wall of Waste A JCB drives at a mound of waste in the recycling plant; broken casing, plastic bags, garden refuse, kitchenware. The great shovel lowers to push back the accumulation causing a wall of fragments to rise up and form a looming silhouette against the gusting sky.

Richmond Bridge A bus moves out past a parked van, squeezing an oncoming car into the roadside. A girl in a black cardigan and jeans hesitates at the crossing, watching the traffic for a space to step out. Builders pass casual conversation leaning against scaffolding props of the dusty renovation. A group of tourists pause to photograph each other before the river view. A middle aged man sits squarely in a dark blue saloon parked on the bridge, reading a map and waving on drivers with a flapping hand. Two women leave the hair salon, attractively presented in flounced summer dresses. Rooftops of redbrick terraces and a scatter of local shops mark the narrow exit over the river to Twickenham.

Part Nine

Vale Of Albion

2005

Paint Can "Still painting then?" The cheerful woman up from the country probes the man with a casual question as he collects a can of yellow emulsion from the local hardware store. "Stuck at the computer all week, I like to do a bit of landscape at the weekend." He mumbles.

Slow Coffee Ramblers at Lulworth Cove sit around the bar waiting for their order. The thin man slowly processes their coffees; a tall glass of latte, cups of frothy expresso. He shuffles between chrome taps, giving an odd squirt of boiling water to top up the cups. Orange juice in tall glasses sits on the tray. The men stare at the objects patiently, not yet ready for serving. The thin man continues to check the details of each cup and gradually turns his thoughts to the issue of the tray. He removes a round paper doily in favour of a square, that better supports the china and glasses. After forty minutes the order appears ready and he indicates to the ramblers the time to remove their goods to the terrace. They exit balancing the tray with care while one remains to pay the bill.

Bad Weather Coming "They're laying on a cold spell next week." A woman reports in the hardware store. "The log man has been cleaned out by panic buyers, frightened the gas may be shut off." Customers listen calmly and one goes outside to stock up with wood and coal.

Leashed Dog "Don't touch the dog!" A young mother steers her children past a leashed mongrel along a street in Swanage. "You don't know where it's been." Across the road some students unload their bikes, scuba gear and body board, shaking out the sand and hike large rucksacks into a dark doorway open between the shops.

Fixings, Wareham "You'll need a counter-sunk device, like a bed fitting." The proprietor of the hardwarec store pays close attention to the customer's sketch and ponders a solution to the construction. He picks through shelves of boxes searching for the right brackets and screws. "Think of the use of a bed, these joints need to be strong enough to stand a shifting pressure. "The man chats amiably. With time in hand the customer turns to view the store, a marvellous and comprehensive collection of practical materials.

Filling Station "No.10, the Volvo." He vaguely indicates the car in the forecourt. The young man swipes the card and passes a slip to sign. "You have a nice weekend." He says. "You too." Comes the response.

Dolphin Inn, Bovey Tracey 04/2006
A shortish man twists his heavy body to negotiate the arms of a leather jacket, then crouches to pick something from the floor. Swaying slightly he approaches the bar to settle his bill.

He twists his body into arms of the leather jacket pulled over a cardigan and cream slacks, before swaying gradually towards the bar. Red anorak, grey trousers, the woman perches on a high bar stool.

Black spiked hair, a beat era style moustacheless beard, black shirt, he notes consecutive customers orders, serving at the bar.

'As soon as I'm able' The girl takes an additional order for mature cheddar and biscuits, with coffee, to follow a full steak meal. She disappears to the kitchen returning with three substantial fish platters.

*Tavistock Marke*t "That's got a good weight to it." The customer jogs the bag with two home-baked traditional loaves of bread, one brown, one white. "You'll know it when you've eaten them," responds the stall holder in a stand just by the court buildings in Tavistock market.

"She'd look good in a bikini." Ragged presentation, grizzled lean weather beaten features, the man in a baseball cap with a poked out ginger ponytail leans in a familiar way on the tea bar, roll up in one hand, remarking on the physical attributes of the owner's wife. "They'd look at her." he leers "Only joking love." He retreats from the burly bearded proprietor with the ketchup to his family at a round table. His substantial wife, also in a baseball cap, thrusts a silver lighter under his nose for the cigarette.

Hay Tor "Naïve of me to roll the car into the snow." The visitor twitters while an expert young man attaches a tow rope to rescue his vehicle. As he swerves shakily back onto the road a bus packed with ramblers rolls sideways to stick in the drift. At Dartmeet children wrap themselves in their father's coat against the cold and play beside the fast running waters of the hill stream.

Store The customer glances at the overhead monitor as items are processed. He notes the quality of tone and colour in the recorded image, that provides an intriguing perspective on the rear of the convenience store.

White Blank white windows illuminated in the evening of the Gents at the edge of a small park, beside the high street of the Devon village.

"I got stuck in a drift on the moors this morning." He begins the story for the proprietor at the bar. "Well that's something." The man responds with a total lack of interest and turns away to another customer. "Well it happened to me." The man says to himself as he returns with a drink to his table for one.

Evening Meal One waitress briefly holds another round the waist as they proceed with purpose towards a new range of customers. The beat of the Harlem Shuffle relays softly over the speakers as a man carefully sections a portion of fish for consumption. The intense tones of *Rescue Me* are heard softly over the speakers as the man raises a glass of beer while chewing steadily on a portion of fish.

He flexes his upper torso under a ribbed white pullover adopting a confident stance beside the seated woman. The large man in a cream ribbed pullover engages the woman in conversation. She leans back slightly in her bar stool and crosses her legs. He talks and sucks a pint of lager, she sips a glass of red wine. Around the bar a man alone reads every inch of the Times, flapping pages noisily as he moves through the paper.

Drift In the early morning a barely perceptible murmur of men's voices below the hotel window.In the early morning the barely perceptible murmur of voices in the street below. The words cannot be distinguished and form an abstract bubble that grows into a mysterious drift, to an interested listener in the first floor room of the Inn.

Shades "Can't read the label," a woman asks the man for assistance as she thumbs through racks of sunglasses at the back of a Boots store. "I think you look here." He indicates a product label and continues to pick and finger from a multitude of styles. 'Have you tried the designer label stand?' His wife intervenes to aid his concentrated search.

Market Day, Fore Street A woman chats to her companion in Fore Street, Totnes. Her hair hangs to her lower back and is braided in tight cork-screws bound with small many coloured ribbons and plaited with daisies. Her dress is also layered; a short jacket of padded velvet inset with beads and buttons is worn over a hand-knitted pullover and lace edged blouse. The rûched skirt dyed dust pink and pale green inter-sected with pale yellow bands. Sturdy legs are cased in ankle socks which tuck in heavy walking boots. Locals mix with visitors on market day in Fore Street, the narrow uphill lane is hung with streamers strung along the old beamed shop fronts. Trestle tables carry trays of collectibles - used books, glassware, toys, candles, home baked biscuits and cakes and jams. A woman wears a large paper daisy in her hair and attached to pixy shoes. She pauses to chat with a lady in Elizabethan costume.

"You don't have time to eat."An irritating child looks up at the visitor as he commences his steak frites and points a stick at him. The boy's indulgent mother chats cow-like with her friends leaving him to his own devices. At another table a bearded man chews with his mouth open still talking, rolling food around on his tongue and filling his cheeks. His son carves up a sandwich wrapped in silver foil for a relative waiting up the road.

"I've a long drive to Cornwall tomorrow." He chats with the receptionist, while thinking about remaining at the hotel to sketch in the gardens.

Smeaton's Pier, St.Ives She, decorative in pale blue shorts and a cream wind cheater. He matches with beige pegs and a light blue anorak. They stand shielding their eyes against the light on the stone jetty, taking in the broad span of Carbis Bay seen from Smeaton's Pier in St.Ives.

Zennor "My bike has twenty two gears." The young man chats with his companions in the tea garden of the Inn at Zennor. "Did you find your tomato?" The hostess pauses by the man who mumbles a response through a thick ham sandwich. "I swallowed it already. I must like tomatoes." He smiles a bread crumbed acknowledgement and resumes a pencil sketch of rooftops of the village.

Waiting A young woman fondles her hair while staring abstracted at a decorative wall hanging in the restaurant. She draws long dark hairs through her fingers and only awakens when her escort returns to the table with lager and red wine.

Dartmouth-Dartington-Penzance 05/2007

Average Things "I don't have real ambitions," the American perches uncomfortably on a tall chrome bar stool, conversing with his female friend in a café in Dartmouth, "I mean I could do what my father does easily. What I'd like is some security but money isn't everything; a home, to see friends, good food, wine, music, you know - average things. It's in the future I guess, when I'm a middle aged man." "You shouldn't just look to the future' says the woman, "you should take pleasure now, in the present." They fall silent, digesting the core of her message and chew on wedges of carrot cake.

Dreaming After driving to various villages he falls asleep in the single ensuite room. He dreams his face is bitten by a large dog when he wakes to his wife's call. His face rests on two fingers of his right hand which has lost its circulation.

Levels He regards levels of foliage of the tall trees shifting in a soft morning breeze as he enjoys a cup of tea on awaking in the single room.

Menu "I would appreciate a dinner prepared by yourselves on my last night." The newly arrived guest invites a menu to the guest house proprietor. "Do you like seafood? We can do a flat sole baked with seasonal vegetables." "Will there be bones?" He enquires. "Not too many." The owner reassures him.

Sculptures "My wife is so busy with her sculptures she is going to employ an assistant." The men converse in the bar of the Yacht Inn in Penzance. "What can I get you?" Another cheerfully joins the group. A woman brings a hot pie with peas to the man who turns his back to hunch over his evening meal.

Mousehole "I'm all out of Victoria Sponge." She informs the visitor and points to the cake cabinet, "But I've still got some lemon drizzle and carrot cake." He chooses carrot cake with a pot of tea for one. While the order is prepared he stares beadily at a dealer working in an adjacent picture shop, and focuses on a detailed oil of apple blossom in Provence, presented in an immaculate swept silver frame. Below the harbour wall a girl makes the face of a cat with circles of multi-coloured stones.

Sennen Cove She laughs girlishly at her companion. "Out to dinner later?" She suggests. He mumbles a low key reply. 'So it's football again then." She grumps. "I'm free to do what I want, any old time." Mick Jagger sings over the speakers in a coffee bar at Sennen Cove.

Orange A girl with an orange scarf wrapped like a turban crosses before a vintners shop near Church Street in Penzance.

Murmurings from the Vale of Albion He takes some tentative steps down the grassy bank to a gravelled path, and follows along to a wicket gate that leads to the headland of Soar Mill Cove. He pauses to regard sheep who graze placidly on the rising hills above the cove, and looks out to the ocean where the small triangle of a yacht sits becalmed in sunlit waters.

San Francisco-Hawaii 08/2006

Empty-Full Through the doors of Saks 5th Avenue on Union Square. San Francisco he glances with a mild interest around the makeup counters, before taking the elevator to the upper floors. He stops at each level to inspect sections of different brands; *Gucci, Armani, Versace, Prada.* His attention is drawn to occasional mannequins, gracefully clothed in sombre tones of grey to black; and intriguing Armani ensemble of a wrap-over top tied with woollen chords and a matching warm grey skirt. Caroline Herrera's section is unattended, it offers a disordered rack of floral print dresses and baggy shapeless trousers; not very appetising. He proceeds to each level to the top where he notes the location of the down escalator as he circles the stalls. A bored assistant, isolated by here stand. Another pair in closed gossip. In mid-afternoon the floors are empty of customers; soft piped music masks a total vacuum. Meanwhile, down the road at H&M the place is threshing with activity. The pay desk with a row of assistants at the tills is barely able to cope with the endless queues of eager girls carrying armfuls of clothes and accessories, while excited clusters of shoppers finger racks of colourful garments with boldly signed discount prices.

Flies "You mixed those drinks perfectly yesterday." The young woman at the beach bar, in a brown beach tunic, floppy felt hat and big shades, catches the barman's attention with some casual conversation. "Will you have a drink?" She offers him. "No he'd be fired on the spot if the management found out," chips in another bar boy. "Really, that's amazing, I didn't know that." Says the girl. "Do you know who she is?"The barman looks shocked at the indication of her power. "Lots of flies here," she turns to her neighbour sipping a soda. "Clean on the rest of the island, but lots of flies around here."

New Guest He places a very battered Louis Vuitton case on the marble counter, takes off his half frame spectacles and presses his nose to the floor plan, scrutinising the rooms offered to his family. His wife, equally serious, receives her black Amex back from the assistant after process. The local girl smile prettily and produces a basket of gifts for their child, which the father takes and places on the floor for her inspection. The child, who wears Ray Ban glasses and an expensive designer print skirt with high heeled gold strap sandals, sorts unsmiling through the selection.

Part Ten

Chronicler

2006

Circle "You are soothing; when you tell your stories it's like slipping into a warm bath." She offers him some personal observations as they share impressions in the circle. "But you are cryptic, evasive. Who are you really?"He twitches defensively entwining his fingers, fidgeting before the listeners who wait his response. "Thank you," he replies "I can learn from what you've said." He tries to explain himself by telling another story but the woman on his left restrains him from continuing further.
"There you go again, covering it all with a sugary layer, making it all safe for you." The moderator intercepts her probing. She starts up in surprise, eyes widening, and arches defensively against a perceived attack. The man also flushes and falls silent, waiting the outcome of the triangular collision within the circle. "My wife is an open book but I like secrets." He chats to the man on the stairway to the exit. "Last week she attacked me over dinner in a restaurant saying, "What are you? Who are you?" "Oh sure," the man replies, "I'll see you next week." He laughs lightly before retreating to the cloakroom.

Whitehall Café He leans on the counter, his right hand sweeping back a long raincoat worn over a dark suit, as he continues a long conversation with the owner on a subject of mutual interest. The waitress serves a salami sandwich and cup of tea to a customer and then stands quietly by the expresso machine regarding the man. She picks up his black homburg hat from the table and waits for a suitable moment to pass it, but he continues to chat in a low tone. An office worker enters and briskly checks the price of cakes in the cabinet, then counts out correct change for his choice. The man at the counter eventually pauses and looks towards the door and takes his hat. Thanking the owner for his time and interest he exits to the avenue of Whitehall.

Queue "I'll bring someone to replace you Maria." The manager flits around the tired girl with dark curled hair at the pay desk. A woman with a double buggy occupies her attention with a purchase which she processes very slowly. At the next till a girl delves in her purse for some change, dipping into a clutch of curled paper receipts, her long slender fingers occasionally retrieving a coin while the assistant makes a tortuously slow reading of her advantage card. To speed the transaction the customer's companion, a weighty ginger haired woman contributes a £5 note, thrust forward with two fingers. In this situation of confused paralysis the queue extends endlessly, and draws heavy impatient breathing from silent and morose shoppers. The first woman finally completes her purchase and moves to leave, but her double buggy is blocked by that of the ginger haired girl. With no apparent leeway they stare at each oer like great inert masses. Eventually the three bodies with their baggage and offspring negotiate a passage past each other in the narrow gangway and very gradually clear from the counter, allowing an exhausted queue to inch a step forward towards service.

Top Model "Hello girls." The tall presenter with bony features, long straight blonde hair and a gash of bright red lipstick greets the contestants with a hard smile and bright eyed stare, drawing herself to a regal bearing to exercise an evaluation of their tasks. Introducing the panel of judges; a bedraggled dark haired Filipino woman, a great fat man of amiable demeanour, and a dry tough faced woman with a rather leaden presence, she proceeds to show the girls their best shots from the recent session with a noted fashion photographer.

They twitter and squeak with anticipation as various over-ripe and stylistically dated images are projected, and convey their gratitude for the experience of the shoot. The judges contribute remarks, both kind and critical, to further define their search for a top model. In the end scene the tall blonde makes a final selection, calling forward five successful entrants and leaving one alone, whose tearful exit from the studio is tracked closely by cameras which graze on her emotional destruction as she packs and prepares to return to nowhere.

Bleak House From the gloomy setting of a mid-Victorian melodrama the watchers compete to identify names of the celebrated cast, whose large and waxen features loom large from the shadows. As the story unfolds with due solemnity chatter in the room diverts to random subjects. By the time tea is made the channel has been switched to a lighter episode of a continuing American teen romance.

Goddess "Yes she is becoming a Goddess." He agrees with the crop haired man who endorses the universal acclaim for the young performer, featured in a film rewrite of a classic novel adapted by an old acquaintance.

Prone The dust covered paramedics crouch in urgent consultation over the prone body of a young woman by a wrecked car in a tunnel concerned for her survival. She twists and turns with boredom ending up face down in the armchair.

Little Britain She twists and turns with boredom, curling face down in the armchair as they view the latest episode of tragedy, accident and death set in a tunnel in the popular hospital series. She then arranges herself in comfort surrounded by cushions on the sofa to concentrate on sketches in the popular comedy series. Her sister intervenes with a story but is waved to silence.

Whine The horn blares repeatedly, a high pitched whine in the night that disturbs the occupant. Looking through the frosting window of the white van he sees the man slumped onto the steering wheel who occasionally lifts and bangs his head on the horn. "Are you drunk mate?" He enquires gently speaking through the half open driver door. "You want to be careful of the police, they'll take your licence away." "S'alright,"he slurs, "I'm waiting for a friend." Gaunt faced with frizzled cropped hair he waves claw like hands to clear away the enquiry. "Turn the engine off and go home on the bus." the resident advises and leaves the man sitting in the van in darkness.

Liquid Wall They discuss the topical news quiz of sophisticated humour they have viewed together. "It's like watching a party from a distance,"he says, "but when we laugh with the panel's responses, they are really laughing at us. It's their party, they are the actors and we are only watching over a great divide. When we turn off the TV we are alone. It's a glass wall." "Quite perceptive but I don't think of it like that," she replies, "It's more like Stargate– the jellied screen the pilots walk through to another dimension." "Yes it's liquid." He agrees.

Presenter Her eyes slant with laughter, wide well-formed cheekbones seem to fill the entire screen. She projects an intense warmth and good humour, entertaining with a flow of adept remarks. She effectively controls the panel of guests, inserting shrewd asides in their lively banter. She confidently holds the centre stage and carries the studio audience with bubbling energy in an expert presentation of the popular and topical news quiz.

2007

Together They view an interactive TV map of locations in Surrey along with related clips of comedians bred there for film and television. 'I wish I was part of a group that wanted me.' She remarks wistfully. He reflects on the ease and confidence of the selected entertainers in occupying the broadcast space. Casualty She rejects his explanation of his conduct and angrily ends their relationship. The door closes and she is seen copiously weeping through shuttered blinds. He returns to his studio to progress a painting of a Paris bridal fashion window, while listening on the radio to an interesting history of the SAS.

Spring "I love days like this," his neighbour perks up over the screen, "Just being outside." "Yes, the spring time," he mutters, hunched over his desk, staring at the monitor.

Flashback The detective and his team interrogate the man who discloses false information about the relative. Numerous flashbacks in black and white follow the story of victims of the last century.

Fat They watch a film with abject horror of the fattest man, following excruciating details picked by the camera of broken patches of skin in his vast billowing calves and the soles of his feet, and his salivating mouth as he gorges a double fried breakfast, also clearing remains of another plates on his companion's behalf.

Give *"**Give!**",* the presenter in an ugly red leather close fitted dress exhorts the passive audience arranged in rows in the studio. Unknown celebs move lumpishly into view with their brief entertainments. Cameras graze on scenes of poverty and destitution filmed out there in the dark continent.

Melrose "Melrose is too queasily confident." They judge the various sized girls lined up in the talent contest.

Artist The senior artist guides two prominent TV news men to favourite master works in the exhibition and the camera closes in on his own confused paintings for comparison. "Such a good looking man," she remarks with approval from the sofa. "He resembles my former accountant." He responds. They then briefly view a report on attacks on women.

Threshing She threshes with dreams of an intimate nature and wakes with a start in her bed. "Somewhat over-egged I think," he grumbles,

"Embroidering Jane Austen for the international market with all this guff." They switch off the period costume drama and retire for the night.

Sagging "Captain Westwood?" Her eyes meet his in long gaze of intense attraction, returned by him with a powerful stifled emotion. Her mouth drops open, as if framing another remark. His jaw continues to clench and sag in bewildered silence, even as another gentleman collects her to join his carriage waiting outside in the rain for an excursion in Bath.

Signal A tall young woman wheels a buggy before his car at the crossing and points officiously at the amber light with a raised right arm and extended forefinger. He responds with a dead eyed stare, head lowered, both hands evenly grasping the wheel.

Drama He rotates his spoon in the empty plastic jelly cup, glancing occasionally at incidents of pain and emotion in a favourite hospital drama.

Spirit She turns to look at him and talks with him, then offers him a glass of wine. But when she turns to look again he has gone. Noting the bolted door she realises he must have been a spirit of her friend who in another shot is shown to have died.

Moments They relax at the end of the evening with a review of one hundred comic moments in television, some of which are occasionally amusing.

Matinée The boy wears a curious fur cap which covers his eyes. He leans forward to his relatives, leering strangely. His mother returns from the kiosk and distributes a variety of sweets and soft drinks which he grabs and consumes. A loud voice booms over the speakers joking with the audience, instructing that mobile phones should be switched off during the performance.

Book Slot He enjoys the mellifluous tone of a reputed American actor who reads extracts of a reputed American essayist in the morning radio book slot.

Panellist "I'd like him to spunk on a biscuit and eat it." The celebrity panellist suggests a test for men in the topical game show. The girl slides down her chair laughing, while making wild criss-cross movements with her arms, trailing fingers over her shoulders and face. She laughs and shouts out as the rest of the panel laugh and point at her. The compère faces the camera, his beady eyes fixed with a slightly deranged expression of concentrated intelligence. He sits rigidly upright, framed against a background colour of searing pink which gradually changes to a mind-blowing cobalt blue.

Neighbour "What a small letterbox you have." The neighbour stands at the door. "For such a large card." Replies the occupier accepting the seasonal envelope.

Competitors "Didn't they do well?" Bruce brings the couple before the judges for appraisal. She lays a plate of salmon bites on dry biscuits along with salami and cheese, houmas and pitta. They adjust themselves to comfortable positions, reclining on matching sofas and sample the plates. "You take away £30.333 each, haven't you done well?" Dale Winton congratulates three excited competitors who clap the audience that claps them.

Willy Wonka They enjoy the remake of Willy Wonka's Chocolate Factory starring Johnny Depp, noting his perfect smile. "They're false of course," the girl informs him about the smooth capped teeth. His head droops back on the arm of the sofa, mouth dropped open. He wakes with a gargled snort half an hour later.

Victor Her arms lock around his neck as the audience roars its approval of the prize. She cries and laughs and holds him tight. He looks pale and tense, and tries to smile as his wife approaches on camera with his children. The wife detaches his dance partner's strong arms from his neck and embraces her. The girl then seizes one of the children and hoists her up to her waist. The presenter waits for an opportunity to present the award, a globe made of glittering mirror plates. Confetti showers over the winning couple, as if marking a victorious marriage.

Grazing The camera moves into close up and grazes lovingly on the features of the Grand Dame of the theatre. In split second frames it plays her lively eyes against the lines drawn tight around her lips and slightly pockmarked skin over her powerful cheek bones. She regards herself in a large mirror, semi-draped, with an expression of poignant self regard for earlier times, and conveys a personal defiance to the encroaching shadows of old age.

Yorkshire They discuss the hazards of driving in the country, standing in the small gangway between offices on the upper level. "Sometimes a car will go over the edge and into the dyke which can be very deep. Drivers have drowned in them." He describes the roads of Yorkshire. "I was going to Higher Moor on Dartmoor and quite suddenly the fog closed in, completely obliterating theroad. I pulled to the side and out of the mist came a Japanese tourist, confused and waving a camera." The other replies.

The Detective The detective pursues an intense line of enquiry into the blood ritual between men of ancient significance. He looks around for some refreshment in the kitchen and settles on a mandarin orange with some sparkling water.

Reflection "You can look now." The stylist in a sharp green dress and platinum framed spectacles places the woman before a tall mirror. She gasps with pleasure as her new image reflects back to her.

Chronicler They sit in the trattoria sharing a plate of houmas and taramasalata. "I feel like a mortuary attendant, recording the activity of others and later attending their internment, carefully brushing the corpse and improving their presentation for eternity. I am a chronicler." "What?" She can't hear him in the general noise. "**C-H-R-O-N-I-C-L-E-R**" He shouts the spelling across the table. She ignores him, looking around at the couples busy with their meals.

Repeat They sit and laugh together at the sophisticated news quiz with its engaging repartée. They join in guessing the picture puzzle of celebrity photos. "But Scottie's dead now, they fired his ashes into space; so this must be a repeat." They fall silent and reflective.

Casualty He turns away and hides his face to avoid the shot of a man's shattered leg with bones sticking out of pulsing flesh. Later the man seems to have recovered quite well, though he is in some emotional difficulty with his daughter who flounces out of the hospital room, giving him an accusing look regarding her boyfriend who lies dead on a neighbouring crash trolley.

The Crew Having enjoyed the latest episode of Dr Who, they continue to view with interest an hour long, detailed programme of explanation of the special effects, delivered with staring eyed energy and enthusiastic laughter by the originator and members of the production team.

They Laugh The detective's rugged features transform into a lurid mask of horror, in vivid shades of red and green. They laugh from the sofa before drifting away from the TV to other little tasks around the house.

As If The girls are confident and lively; of healthy stock, well built, even fleshy; with doe like eyes and smooth, well kept hair, carefully dressed. The young men however, are strangely unsatisfactory; of an unkempt presentation, lanky, inarticulate, greasy hair over the eyes in an old fashioned style of the late 1960s. The girls seem to like them all the same and eagerly join in intimate embraces with long glutinous kisses. The mother, a weighty creature, is also avidly involved with the scenes of domestic entanglement, and obviously appreciates the young men's presence in the house.

TV Couple "How are you darling?" The imposing blonde enters the hospital room, trailed by a camera crew, to collect her sickly husband, who crouches faint and nauseous in a chair after the severe illness. A back shot scans the surface of her tanned shoulder of massive strength, and comes back into focus on her little husband beyond, pale and delicate in a white nylon T shirt and baseball cap, crouched over a china bowl, ready to vomit.

Bambi Pale faced and wide eyed the pretty fair haired girl from Liverpool smiles luminously at the camera. The senior woman guides her through tests for the catwalk. "A face lift?" They note the slanted eyes and smooth cheekbones with taut shiny skin. The young girl bubbles excitedly, visiting a LA trash fashion store, as she is loaded with bags of free promotional merchandise.

Expert The taller woman pushes her hawk like features right in close to the quivering face of the more timid lady boutique owner in Banstead, Surrey. The woman flinches with fright under the aggressive approach, but regains her poise with a nervous little smile. She is shown later expressing profound gratitude for the expert's guidance, to the benefit of her business. She stalks into the boutique in tight slacks and killer heels. She presses her bony features close up to the shorter blonde woman's fearful face to confront her taste and presentation. The camera roves the shop, focusing telling frames on sundry old age pensioners who shuffle around amidst disordered racks and piles of stale knitwear, and old fashioned dresses.

Low Life "Do you want one? I'll give you one!" The stocky grizzled cyclist screams at another who blocks his path. "Low life," comes a muted response. Further enraged the cyclist hops up and down on his seat. "Low life." the other steadily repeats, driving him incandescent with rage.

Savants A fat man, mentally disabled with spots around his chin, dark greasy hair and owl frame glasses, reaches for a book from a library shelf. "He is able to memorise five hundred pages in an hour from one sight reading." The breathless voice-over confirms. Another, bearded, introverted, plays a piano with intense concentration. "He can hear a whole concert and then play it from memory." The breathless voice-over adds.

Car Robot Metal parts soar skyward and fly about in time to an exciting musical beat. They come together, reforming as a giant robot. The mechanical creation strides across the city and then disperses, reforming again as a smart new car which is rotated for inspection.

Alter Ego He reels from the impact of dozens of bullets, spurting blood drenches his clothes. Eventually after some resistance he collapses and expires. Later he magically reappears as his alter ego, who has survived, and embraces his wife outside their stately home. In the closing scene of the final episode he meets his aged mother who turns out to be a vampire, baring an impressive row of fangs.

Fat Lips The girl weeps in the dock as she recounts the suspicious drowning of a man. 'She has very big lips' They observe, "Perhaps an implant?" They continue to watch her unusual features with interest.

Da Vinci Code "Do it!" She shouts from the sofa as Audrey Tatou looks meaningfully into Tom Hanks' eyes. But he only respectfully kisses her forehead before departing to stay at a glamorous Parisian hotel; from where he goes out into the night to follow the sign of the rose in the final scene of the film.

Visions He touches the person and immediately sees visions of violent incidents; the brutal murder of a girl in a forest, the scene emanating from a swirling vortex of computer graphics. The landlady of a B&B in Manchester is obviously attracted to his lean and tense physique and after a drink indulges his pleasure, her mountainous form rearing and bucking above his delicate frame. "Shield your eyes." The viewer advises present company from the armchair. The lady detective also seems attracted to his lean and tense physique, and she swallows two whiskies to relax herself for an encounter. His ex-wife also regards him fondly, as does his young daughter. "A possible star vehicle," the viewer comments from the armchair, "reminiscent of Tom Courtenay in *"The Loneliness of The Long Distance Runner."* He adds expertly.

Crossing He slows to a halt at the crossing and waits while a young woman in a pink top hesitantly puts one foot on the road, while continuing a conversation on her mobile phone. Eventually she reaches the other side and halts and turns back to face the way she came, still in conversation on her mobile phone.

Market Day Thriving with activity the busy market place includes themed international stands, French and German, offering an array of baked goods and preserved meats; glazed tarts, long salamis, cheeses, baskets of biscuits. A cone roofed bar serves steyns of lager to local residents, perched on high stools from where they check their children who rush in and out of jets of water that shoot up at intervals in a central area.

Roll A tissue loosely gathered in a winding white loo roll. Yellow plastic bottles, of moisturiser and conditioner. A female razor propped vertically. Assorted objects on the flat top of the cistern in the ensuite facility.

Ladies Lunch At a busy café in North London four women gather for lunch, each forking substantial mouthfuls of salad from deep wooden bowls, chatting, smoking and padding dribbling mouths with serviettes.

Rich Today "£35million, lucky woman." He reads the headline in stark white on black along with her chirpy round face centred in cartoon graphic signs of success: expensive cars, champagne, desirable travel destinations. "Perhaps, or perhaps not." He mumbles to the two Polish girls in the East Twickenham barber shop as he settles up for the cut.

Older-Younger "My God look at that." They stare at crepulous folds of fat that roll down over the panty line, scooped up and kneaded by the presenter's fingers like rolls of dough. They shield their eyes in horror as the camera moves across the rippling surface of her lower legs, marking lumps of clogged veins that protrude under the skin. "Now look at yourself." The stylist invites the woman to open her eyes to the mirror set up on the piazza of a sunny continental resort. She gasps with pleasure at her new beauty, and is then filmed frolicking in the waves with her grateful husband. "That is incredible." they murmur from the sofa.

Ray "I just love these shoes, I picked them up for fifty euros in Paris." The camera brings a pair of gold sequinned pumps into focus and scans slowly up black velvet trousers to a green halter top, to rest on the bright smile of the vivacious Hollywood star: Summer from OC. On the Discovery Channel shoals of fishes swirl away from the diver, dipping in and out of sunbeams filtering the ocean, that catches multi-coloured patterns and silver gleams. A vast white Manta Ray floats across our view and away into enveloping shadows.

Airplane 18/08/2007 They crouch sweating and stiff in their premier economy seats, switching channels for entertainment. Star Guide Hollywood parades leading young beauties. "She was so right to choose the pale green dress." Misha Barton twirls prettily, arching her neck for a perfect camera angle. Fishes swirl in among the corals, beams of sunlight catching multi-coloured fins. A silvery ghost sweeps past, over the diver, a great white Ray with a long stinging tail. "**Oh shit!**" The engineer's wife in an adjacent seat shouts as her baby tumbles from a flight cot, launching another spate of grating screams.

Mauritius 07/2007

Flic en Flac "What pretty colours on the houses." He remarks as they drive through a rather battered township in Mauritius. Villas are painted cream with bright blue tiled roofs. At a turning random walls of a carpet warehouse are picked out in blocks of orange, lilac and mint green. Among casual groups of bystanders a striking woman with dark brown hair falling over lean features, elegant in a black and gold embroidered sari. At the junction to the resort a fit youth with peroxide crop and small gold earring, annoyed to have missed the bus, shouts to his companion. A tall muscular man in a hooded jacket lurches towards the taxi and the occupants shrink back, as if he might climb in, but they ramble off elsewhere.

James "James, I like that, it sounds like a famous name..James." The staff member tittle tattles as he guides the new party to their accommodation after a welcome tropical fruit drink.

Front Desk "Do you organise tours?" He addresses the young man at reception who stares blankly. He vaguely gestures to a colleague busy with another. "Can you change rands into rupees?" A woman in black enquires, then pushes her stocky husband forward to press the matter with the young man who wavers blankly. They shrug and move off to the bar area.

She Walks Past Soft and weighty form contained in a light green sarong, the wreath of material tied tight around her waist, a slight overlap of tanned flesh at the middle. She returns with fresh towels to relax on her sundeck with her holiday novel.

Greeting How Are You? Three senior women and gentlemen greet by the pool. One in a brown silk top with gold chains and black pegs, legs slightly bowed at the thigh, and a lady in turquoise with tight fitting white pants.

She Walks Past A cascade of dark auburn curls falling over strong tanned shoulders, determined eyes shaded by designer glasses. A lightweight strappy black top and matching pantaloons, brown calves, feet cased in white gold buckled sandals.

Morning Exercise The pretty French woman cheekily splashes the instructor and laughs. He responds, kicking a spray of water back at her and adopts a new pose for their exercise .in the pool, stepping in time to the continuous beat. He raises one arm and grabs his back foot bending it behind at the knee and stretches the calf. The line of women watch and try to imitate his action with difficulty. A man watching from the side crosses his arms over his shoulders and twitches in time to the music, flicking his feet stiffly in the water.

He Walks Past Bare headed in only pale blue trunks in the cool breeze of a grey morning. Pads barefoot along by the pool, returning with a towel, book and a strappy black top for his partner.

She Walks Past Cropped boyish hair, spectacles, orange T-shirt.

Sugar Club Three Indian women in black and gold saris, play each other at snooker in a low roofed cabin. Giant chess pieces are set out in the open area. Ladies file up steps to book their beauty treatments. A local man holds a disconnected telephone, whiling away time in casual conversation with the sports desk.

Choices They browse the many dishes on offer in a buffet presentation, octopus salads, banana mayonnaise, chicken and pineapple. The many choices leading to a main course of curry and Chinese dishes, They add spinach and noodles to loaded plates and then explore desserts; little coconut cakes, chocolate mousse, banana and apple fritters, crêpes smeared with chocolate sauce.

He walks past Tall, fresh, clear even features, fringe of smooth hair flops over forehead. Black sports outfit, banded T-shirt and loose bottoms, white and black trainers. He walks past carrying a saucer of cheese, salami and fruits to his breakfast table.

Three men laugh Posing for a photo by the gun-whale, and bare their chests for the woman who joins them. One rolls up his t shirt dancing to the beat, shows his chest tattooed in gothic script: Christine. The older man leaves the bar with a Coke, another in a cheesecloth head wrap collects two waters. The crew haul anchor to return to the bay.

Dolphin Watch She tenses in kneeling by the bowsprit, presenting a broad rear as she adjusts to a comfortable position. The crew adjust the winding gear of the fore sail and catamarans and small craft converge in the shallow waters to follow the occasionally bucking dolphins.

Waiting The woman in a party of four dips a finger of toast in her boiled egg and then in a small pool of syrup in a saucer. a boy hovers with a flask of coffee and bends forward to refresh her cup, one arm behind his back. At the counter the staff stack used dishes and cutlery, scraping remains into a bucket, then laying knives and forks in orderly layers on stacked plates. A woman of senior rank hovers by the boy monitoring his activity and sends him out again into the tables to check for finished meals. Cups are left for later clearance.

She walks past White pullover casually draped over grey sweat shirt wrapped at an angle on her shoulders, a soft bag slung on the left arm. Khaki shorts on healthy brown calves, in white socks and plimsolls. Hair tied back with a red ribbon; confident relaxed pose, even walk, on the way to the beach.

Fish landing station 'Squidy' in turquoise blue letters on white hull with scattered black painted ink blots for illustration; a parked wooden boat at the fish landing station. Red crested cockerels and hens peck about in the dry grass. A white dog pads over the foreshore towards a pair of women with their children looking for shells in the sand. A group of four men chat together, killing time in the heat of midday.

Blue House He gets up stiffly from the stone bench and stretches and turns to regard the deep blue wall of a building fretted with white verandas at the back, a small rear door marks the exit of a street front store selling beach wear.

Sand, shale and grit He looks down as he walks to avoid eye contact with locals, and the stream of taxis that slow and honk twice for a pickup. Uneven surface of the roadside is composed of tough dry grass, with patches of white shale, red earth, sand and grit. A low wind breathes through the trees planted at wide intervals, strung out along the common land by public beaches.

Clearing The member of maintenance staff carefully positions his implement to pick up dry foliage and place it into a black garbage bag suspended in a container of a small chrome edged trolley.

Clearing 2 A lady of the waiting staff circulates the breakfast tables, attending guests and clearing used plates promptly. These are stacked on small folding decks and then removed by another to the kitchen.

Daily News He raises a mild query about the daily paper, not delivered, with the woman in the beach shop, and is surprised by the intense and precise quality of her response.

Animated A bald man turns towards his wife. "There is a big debate whether Tom wants to swim or not." He refers to two small children in animated discussion by the pool.

They walk past A bulky couple, he in navy swimwear, matching T-shirt, white stripe, shades, matching baseball cap and sandals, she in an orange outfit. They amble at a steady pace around the pool, a significant bulk lending imposing strength and assurance to their presence.

Bird Song A low breeze wafts the small open window of the cubicle and sunlight breaks occasional slats with pale beams. He hears the chink of crockery cleared from the breakfast tables and birds cheep as he bends over, exerting his every effort in the primary motion of the day.

Frogs A young woman skips gaily into a lit up chalet followed by her handsome partner. Out in the darkness the roar of bullfrogs mating in the lily pond.

Beach Riders Three riders appear, horses with children waked by a guide up from the beach, and walk across the lawn of the settlement. A low breeze waves fronds of palm trees in the fading light. A uniformed sentry sits in a conical roofed box, guarding the boundary of the hotel.

She Walks Past A young girl in black shorts, pale blue shirt casually draped over shoulders, a controlled relaxed attitude, arms folded across her chest; walking towards the beach over thick meshed grass, and beyond a group of boys kicking a football back and forth before the sunlit ocean.

Driver "It is very troubled." The Afghan driver looks down for a moment, both hands on the wheel, as they touch on his home land. "I am taking a holiday to visit my wife's relatives in Uzbekistan , it has a beautiful landscape -Tashkent." "My daughter is visiting Poland and plans to cross the border to Russia." The man replies. "Don't you go there." He continues with stories of mafia killings. "My friend left his family and the village to look for work. They found out about him in the new place, robbed his cash and then shot him dead." They fall silent and look bleakly at the trail of evening traffic to Hounslow. "I love London, it is a wonderful city." The driver adds a positive note.

The North The respected commentator's features jar and are slightly dislocated in the internet broadcast from the icy northern floes. A conversation with the Norwegian ambassador yields interesting insights of international relations in the competed territory.

Pink Tie "Look how he has left his jacket open, he is proud of his pink tie and wants to show it." She remarks, approving the handsome news anchor who swivels about in his chair; intelligently engaged with an American expert in points of a massacre.

Nottingham Hard Rock "She's only wearing panties and a corset." She points out a girl standing behind a column in the bar. Shrieks rise from a gaggle of girls at a long table to the rear.

Real "Real apple pie." a low breathy female voice over encourages attention to the image of vast gleaming prongs of a silver fork which descends with a gentle but meaningful pressure, to gradually break the sugar dusted coating of a gigantic many layered pastry. The metal shafts force a fissure in the yielding substance, penetrating with driving power to disclose a core of soft chunks of pale apple that melt glowingly in its path. Glossy drips of leaking fluid add lustre to its succulence, making the mouth water in anticipation of the glorious dessert that radiates from the plasma screen into a darkened domestic interior.

The '60s "I'm your sister." She regards him steadily. He stares back vacantly, long greasy hair flops over his eyes, just like the '60s.

Baby "Here we go." They follow the action from the sofa, predicting the violent shouting exit of the young girl with her boyfriend and baby in tow, loaded with buggy and bags of nappies. "Oh no." They chorus from the sofa, anticipating a revelation of an emotional nature between the two young people.

Space "Give her some space." The older woman restrains the man from going to the whey faced girl out in the misty garden, who just lost a child.

Rebus "You knew!" The detective accuses the woman of her involvement with an indicated man. She stares up at him from the bed, her gap toothed mouth sagging. "Joanna Watson." She recognises the actress from the sofa.

Britz "I think you're lovely." She gives him an intense look then lowers her eyes modestly, having betrayed her feelings. He looks mildly surprised but then the two secret agents lean towards each other and kiss, the actors making sucking sounds as they engage with each other, glutinously.

King and Queen "Ann." King Henry VIII looks intensely at the brunette actress who performs Ann Boleyn, and moves to kiss her, while trailing a finger down her left breast.

Borat "That's outrageous." They chorus from the sofa as Borat invites an American hostess to assist his bodily functions in the rest room. They appreciate the ingenuity and courage of his comical interventions. He lies back on the sofa and reflects on his unfolding days and closing nights, while faintly amused by revelations of local prejudice by the skilled performer.

Dead-Not Dead In a frightening end scene the tall female interrogator injects the elegant blonde spy woman in the neck with a lethal serum and she dies. Then, surprisingly, at her funeral she revives and sits up in her coffin, and holds her handsome colleague's hand affectionately. The episode ends and there are some clips of the next episode in the series.

The Top "I am in constant touch with all aspects of the fashion industry, the advertising agents, the buyers, photographers." The revered designer fields gentle questions from the arts commentator who gurgles respect-fully, his cowed form dazzled by the celebrity shrinks to the margins of the frame. "I am not like an isolated designer." The star continues. The crew visits small craft manufactories in the back streets of Paris, filming senior women engaged in jewelled fancy pieces, and they interview an old shoe maker, master of his craft.

Half Dream His mind swirls in a half dream as he animatedly describes his life and research to a cluster of interested dinner party guests, but he wakes in silence.

Two Women Their clothes are sensibly chosen for the excursion; dull denim jackets, plain trousers, and both wear heavy thick soled walking boots with rolled down socks. "There's lots of seasonal work," her voice is drowned out by a rising roar of the train going through a tunnel. "..in Austria." She completes her information. Suddenly the two blondes gain a greater dimension; they appear as great mythic sculptures, placid and statuesque in their slight shifting movements - Goddesses. The roar of the underground train lends a dramatic background and they loom large as a genuinely exciting presence in the carriage. They rise up and exit at Green Park, their place is taken by a rather scraggy individual, a thin man with dark curled hair, but there is something to his lean and feral features worth noting; his uneven crumpled figure in the seat and the darting suspicious looks he gives his fellow passengers.

One Size Larger "Batteries?" The man's enquiry is answered by a directing wave from the ginger haired fat boy at the cash desk. "Would you say this is size for size?" He places the tiny disc against a likely replacement. Another customer, a rangy exhausted looking man, collars a girl to present a complaint. "Though it states itself as the proper fitting, this is clearly inaccurate. The part should have been one size larger." He waves the packet about and insists on a switch. At the till the fat ginger boy forces a card for the fourth time into a chip and pin unit, while the customer leans forward to track the transaction. The man presents his minute £1.19 battery for payment and flourishes a £20 note. He fumbles the change and receipt while noting the lack of a bag provided for his purchase.

Lights As darkness falls suddenly lights jn a car parked in a lane by the riverside. A couple is illuminated closeted in an intense conversation. "What is their story?" the man ponders as he cycles by.

The Author

Nicholas James studied painting at the Slade School of Art, UCL and History of Art (MA) at Kingston University. A writer, editor and publisher, his recent assignments have included interviews and reviews of Yinka Shonibare, Marc Quinn, Matthew Barney and others, (*artslant.com*). The editor of Cv/VAR archive and editions, he is presently working on a book: *Curators and Collections: Foundations and Initiatives* and a DVD, *Art Source: documents and editions, 1995-2010.*

For catalogue information of Cv titles in print contact:
Cv Publications . 10 Barley Mow Passage .
Chiswick . London . W4 4PH UK
Tel: +44(0)20 8400 6160
www.tracksdirectory.ision.co.uk